Delius
A life in pictures

Lionel Carley
Robert Threlfall

Thames Publishing
14 Barlby Road London W10 6AR

In memory of
PHILIP EMANUEL

I don't claim to be a
British composer

FREDERICK DELIUS

Childhood and youth, 1862–84

Fritz Theodor Albert Delius was born on 29 January 1862 at no. 6
Claremont, a pleasant street only a few minutes' walk from the centre
of Bradford, in Yorkshire, and just on the edge of the moors.

Bradford was a key centre of the wool trade, and its rapid expansion
through the first part of the nineteenth century brought with it the
squalor of ugly mills and smoking chimneys, but also an affluence
founded on the wealth of wool and allied manufactures.

The house in the background is no. 6 Claremont.

Bradford in 1860, from the Cemetery Terrace.

Julius Friedrich Wilhelm Delius, wool and noil merchant, had established his now-prosperous business in mid-century after emigrating to England from his native Bielefeld, in Germany.

My father loved music intensely and used to tinker on the piano when he knew he was alone. He was a great concert-goer and he often had chamber-music in his house.

He married Elise Pauline Krönig, also from Bielefeld, in 1856.

My mother was not musical at all, but she had great imagination, and was rather fantastically inclined. She was very romantic . . .

Shortly after the birth of Fritz the Deliuses moved back into no. 1 Claremont, the family home that they had briefly vacated while it was being enlarged.

WILLIAM ROTHENSTEIN
Delius, as a boy, used to play with my mother
[an amateur pianist]—his parents were friends
of my parents—

PHILIP HESELTINE
Julius Delius would often entertain at his house the
artists who came to Bradford to give a public concert;
and musical soirées at Claremont were of frequent
occurrence. Joachim and Piatti were among the
musicians . . .

Dr. Joachim, who played at the Delius
family house.

**Fritz was the second son, and fourth child,
of a family of fourteen.**

**Music was encouraged in the house from an
early age.**

*I cannot remember the first time when I began to
play the piano: it must have been very early in
my life. I played by ear, and I used to be
brought down in a little velvet suit after dinner
to play for the company.*

Bradford in the 1870s.

Ilkley: the Old Bridge.

Industrial Bradford pushed ever outward, but the nearby countryside provided a sharp and healthy contrast for young Fritz to explore.

CLARE DELIUS
I shall always think of [him] as standing out against the vivid background of the Yorkshire moors.

I loved riding over the moors to Ilkley—then only a tiny village—where we often spent the summer.

When I was six or seven, I began taking violin lessons from Mr. Bauerkeller, of the Hallé orchestra, who came over from Manchester especially to teach me . . .

My first great musical impression was hearing the posthumous Valse of Chopin which a friend of my father's played for me when I was ten years old. It made a most extraordinary impression on me. Until then, I had heard only Haydn, Mozart and Beethoven, and it was as if an entirely new world had been opened up to me. I remember that after hearing it twice I could play the whole piece through from memory.

The next great thrill I got was when I heard Wagner's music. It was the Walkürenritt played by the Hallé orchestra.

Ilkley Moor.

The schoolboy.

After a spell at a local preparatory school, Fritz was enrolled in 1874 as a pupil at Bradford's Grammar School, a newly-built and stark monument of the Victorian Gothic age.

Bradford Grammar School.

WILLIAM ROTHENSTEIN

The Bradford Grammar School was a dreary building, inside and out . . . The class-rooms, with their shabby, bare walls, ugly stained desks and hot pipes, smelt close and stuffy . . . Yet the school had a great reputation for the number of University Scholarships won there each year, and it attracted many boys from the neighbouring towns.

An enduring love of cricket was already well developed, and summer holidays when sporting and musical tastes could both be indulged were particularly happy periods.

We always spent six weeks at Filey so I used to go over to Scarborough to see the Cricket Festival. How we looked forward to the day when we started from the Midland Station in a special saloon carriage for the seaside!

I saw a match in which 'W. G.' and E. M. Grace played against 18 of the Bradford team. George Ulliot, Bradford's professional, bowled 'W. G.' middle stump and so was given a sovereign by Mr. Priestman who was playing for Bradford. I often attended county matches in the district . . .

W. G. Grace, the great cricketer.

A summer holiday début in 1879.

In 1878 Fritz began a two-year course of study at the International College, a progressive school situated in Isleworth, then a rural London suburb. For the first time came regular opportunities to attend concert and opera performances in London.

CLARE DELIUS

It was towards the end of his schooldays at Isleworth that he composed his first song, bringing it home with great pride for me to sing . . . I remember it began 'When other lips shall speak', and was in two parts, the first for a man's voice and the second for a woman's.

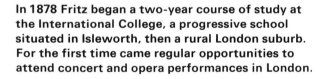

International College, Isleworth.

The early 1880s were marked by a series of travels on behalf of Delius and Company, with Fritz representing his father's firm as a first step towards embarking on a career in the family business.

Stroud.

Stroud, in Gloucestershire, and Chemnitz, in Saxony, were two of his early bases.

PHILIP HESELTINE
. . . in Chemnitz . . . violin lessons were continued with Hans Sitt, who was later on to become Delius's violin-master at the Leipzig Conservatorium.

Hans Sitt. 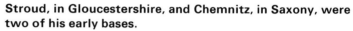Chemnitz.

Most of his trips were to other centres of the wool trade in Europe. Business in Saint-Étienne, however, proved less attractive than visits to Monte-Carlo and Paris; and his uncle Theodor's cultured life-style in the French capital opened his eyes to a wider and more sophisticated world.

Theodor Delius.

The Casino at Monte-Carlo.

Saint-Étienne.

8

Business took him as far north as Stockholm and Norrköping in Sweden, but it was the first experience of Norway that made the most lasting impression.

Stockholm: Port and Old Town.

Jotunheim landscape, Norway.

THOMAS BEECHAM
The influence of the scenic grandeur of the Scandinavian peninsula, particularly the western extremity of it, was profound, mystical and indelible. For the first time he realized his own secret affinity with high and lonely places.

Norrköping.

America and Leipzig, 1884–88

Seeking now to escape from a business career Delius prevailed on his father to back him as an orange planter in Florida.

On 2 March 1884 he left Liverpool for New York on the Cunard Liner *Gallia*, together with his partner in the enterprise, Charles Douglas, also from Bradford.

The *Gallia.*

The journey to Florida ended on the shores of the wide St. Johns River. The orange farm that Julius Delius had purchased was known as Solana Grove and much of it was covered with dense semi-tropical vegetation.

Right. 'Palm Trees, St. Johns River, Florida', by Winslow Homer (detail).

Delius and Charles Douglas.

I was also in the wilderness in Florida, and have since never been able to live long in a crowd.

I was demoralised when I left Bradford for Florida . . . In Florida, through sitting and gazing at Nature, I gradually learnt the way in which I should eventually find myself . . .

Panorama of Jacksonville.

Regular steamers plied the river, and Delius was soon able to make visits to the nearest important town, Jacksonville, 35 miles downriver to the north.

St. Johns River Steamer, *City of Jacksonville.*

Delius's house on Solana Grove.

View of East Bay Street, Jacksonville.

The climate and the flowers are extraordinary and the situation of my grove is lovely and right on the beautiful St John's River . . . The scenery is lovely and I should say remarkably well adapted for a painter. There is a nice little house on the place with a broad verandah facing the St John's river and standing in the middle of the orange trees. In front of the house is a garden with gardenias hibiscus and a few other tropical flowers of which I do not know the names. Over the verandah an enormous honey-suckle creeps and in front of the house to the right and near the river an enormous live oak stands and shades a sort of lawn of very green grass.

Negroes are certainly the most musical people in America. Sitting on my plantation in Florida on the verandah after my evening meal I used to listen to the beautiful singing in 4 part harmony of the negroes in their own quarters at the back of the orange grove. It was quite entrancing . . .

Solana Grove.

Charles Douglas, Delius's partner, did not stay long at Solana Grove. His place was taken for some months by Thomas Ward, a professional musician then in Jacksonville for his health. Apart from being congenial company Ward exerted a distinct musical influence on the younger man.

Thoughts of becoming a prosperous orange farmer gradually receded as Delius became acquainted with musical society in Jacksonville. A piano had been delivered to the grove and the first serious attempts at composition now preoccupied him.

Some years later his first published work appeared in Jacksonville.

Exercises (1884) and sketches for part-songs in a notebook dating from the Florida years.

As far as my composing was concerned, Ward's counterpoint lessons were the only lessons from which I ever derived any benefit.

In the autumn of 1885 Delius moved to Danville, Virginia, a centre of the tobacco industry. Where he had earlier listened attentively to the singing of the Negro plantation workers, now the choruses he heard came from the tobacco stemmeries.

Initially tutor to the two daughters of John Frederick Rueckert (a grandson of the German poet), Delius soon started to teach music at the Roanoke Female College and discovered that for the first time music could make him a modest living.

Gertrude.

John Frederick Rueckert.

Blanche.

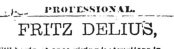

—Prof. Fritz Delius assisted by the interesting Rueckert Quartette and vocal talent, expect to give some classical concerts during the winter which will be free to all students in music in our midst. They will not only be very enjoyable but all very instructive to those attending them.

Left Advertisement in the *Danville Register*, 3 October 1885. *Right* From the *Danville Register*, 6 October 1885.

Roanoke Female College, Danville.

Virginia Ann Watkins, a favourite pupil
and early sweetheart of Delius at the
College.

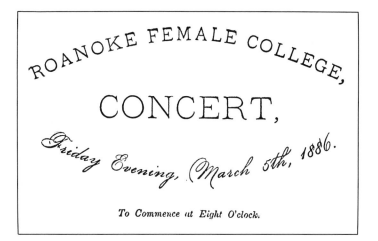

ROANOKE FEMALE COLLEGE,

CONCERT,

Friday Evening, March 5th, 1886.

To Commence at Eight O'clock.

~~⁕PROGRAM.⁕~~

————•◄•►•————

Jubilee Overture. Op. 59. . . . • . . . . . *Weber.*

1ST PIANO.   (Arranged for two pianos, eight hands.)   2ND PIANO.

MR. PHIFER.   MISS AVERETT.
MISS L. MOORE.   MISS L. LIPSCOMB.

Songs. . . . . • . • . . . . . *Franz.*
Spring Night in Norway. Op. 48, No. 6.
Parting. Op. 11, No. 1.
The Spring of Love. Op. 14, No. 5.

MISS P. B. AVERETT.

Concerto for Violin. Op. 64. . . . . *Mendelssohn.*
Allegro molto vivace. (Last movement.)

MR. FRITZ DELIUS.

Trio for Female Voices : "The Dragon Flies." . . , . . . *Bargiel.*

MISSES S. BARNARD, V. WINSTON and P. B. AVERETT.

Programme including a performance by
Delius at the College.

MRS BELLE PHIFER

Mr. Fritz Delius charmed all of us. He was very modest, and he was liked
by everyone because of his nice manners . . . My husband was looked upon
as the leading musician in Danville—in fact, he really established the
classical movement in Danville, and Mr. Delius was directed to him. On
hearing him play, Mr. Phifer was at once conscious of a musical ability of
the first water, and their friendship was almost immediate. He spent most
of his time at our house. My husband secured him a position in the
college, and he did very well there. He also had private pupils, and he gave
French and German lessons in several private houses.

ROBERT PHIFER

I . . . recall the talented young friend of the old years in North Danville.

Robert Phifer, closest friend in Danville.

15

The extensive travels of the 1880s continued. Delius's next goal was the Leipzig Conservatorium, and in June 1886 he left the New World for the Old, arriving (after a brief visit to Bradford) in Leipzig in August, in good time to enrol—with his father's grudging consent—for the fresh academic year.

I have a quartett at my lodgings every Sunday morning. A fine violinist, cellist and viola, I play the piano. It is indeed very enjoyable. We play Schumann, Beethoven, Mozart, Haydn etc.

At Leipzig.

The Conservatorium: Concert Hall.

Delius's foremost teachers at Leipzig were Jadassohn, Reinecke and Sitt, but he quickly grew impatient with formal teaching and was to find that the friendship he established in Leipzig with Grieg, towards the close of 1887, was the most enduring legacy of these two years.

A card party at Leipzig: *l to r*, Nina Grieg, Edvard Grieg, Johan Halvorsen, Delius, Christian Sinding.

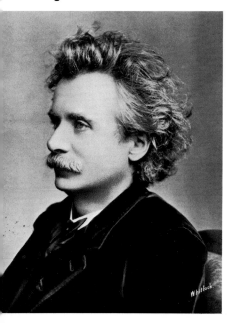

To EDVARD GRIEG   *I tell you frankly, I have never in my life met a nature that has won all my love as yours has done. In my life I have been left to my own resources so much that without realising it I have become selfish and have only usually bothered about myself and worked for myself. You are the only man who has ever changed that and drawn my whole attention to you yourself and aroused the feelings which I now have for you.*

EDVARD GRIEG
Your manuscripts were a pleasant surprise, they were indeed stimulating and I detect in them signs of a most talented composer in the grand style, who aspires to the highest goal . . .
It is my most fervent wish that you will one day receive in your own country the recognition which you deserve, and that you will acquire the material means towards the achievement of your splendid ideal; I do not doubt for a moment that you will succeed.

Title page of the autograph MS of *Paa Vidderne* **melodrama.**

Strongly influenced by the Scandinavians in his Leipzig circle, he turned to Norwegian and later to Danish poets for inspiration, and two of his earliest dedications were to Edvard and Nina Grieg.

EDVARD GRIEG to FRANTS BEYER
Such a Christmas Eve! Indeed, had you been with us you would have said that you would never experience a finer or more interesting one!— First Halvorsen played Hallinger and Springere [*folk dances*], and then Sinding and Halvorsen a suite by Sinding in the old style . . . Then I played with Halvorsen my 2nd Violin sonata, then Nina sang songs by Sinding and me, then Mr Delius played a piano piece which he calls 'Norwegian Sleigh-ride' with the greatest of talent . . . We broke up at 2.30.

EDVARD GRIEG to FRANTS BEYER
This English-American, deeply musical, splendid Hardangervidde-man . . . You must get to know him. He is like us in nothing except feeling! But in the end that's everything!

The album of five songs dedicated to Nina in 1888 was to be his first publication in England, where it appeared in 1890.

Delius left Leipzig in the spring of 1888. His first major composition had been the *Florida* suite (1887), and Sitt had given the work in full with a rehearsal orchestra early in 1888 at Leipzig.

CHRISTIAN SINDING, from Leipzig
You cannot imagine how much I miss you. I have hardly ever before met a person I could trust so completely . . .

Returning to his family in Bradford, he arranged a meeting between his father and Grieg, who was then in London. Grieg strongly recommended a career in music, and Delius now left England for Paris convinced that he could become a successful composer—and with an annual allowance in his pocket.

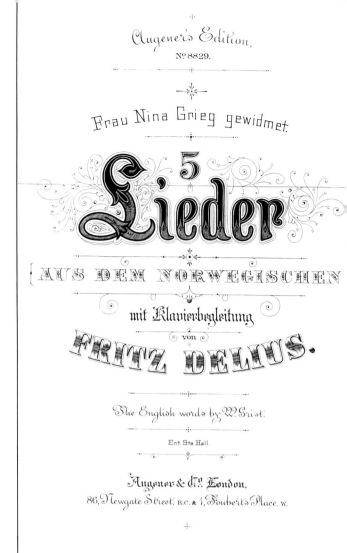

Augener's Edition,
Nº 8829.

Frau Nina Grieg gewidmet.

5 Lieder

AUS DEM NORWEGISCHEN

mit Klavierbegleitung
von
FRITZ DELIUS.

The English words by W. Grist.

Ent. Sta. Hall.

Augener & Cº. London.
86, Newgate Street, E.C. & 1, Foubert's Place, W.

With his sisters in Bradford.

Paris, 1888–99

In Paris Delius stayed for the first months at the home of his uncle Theodor, at no. 43 rue Cambon, a short distance from the Opera.

Caricature of André Messager by Gabriel Fauré.

I have now settled down a bit here and I must confess it pleases me very much. There is something in the atmosphere that is quite different from Germany or England. Life and existence here is remarkable, one cannot but think that every street urchin enjoys life . . . It is beautiful, very beautiful here but I must soon have some quiet. I heard a new opera by Lalo at the Opera Comique, but found it quite empty. Also Aida in the big opera house, quite excellent.

N D. Phot.

Paris: The Opera.

PHILIP HESELTINE
André Messager, whom he frequently met at his Uncle Theodor's house, used to express his liking for Delius's fairy opera *Irmelin* in the most cordial manner.

After a summer break spent in Bradford and Brittany he settled in Ville d'Avray, just outside Paris, on the lakeside where Corot had until 1875 lived and painted. One of his closest friends during these early years in France was the Norwegian violinist, Arve Arvesen, also fresh from Leipzig.

A *Petite Suite d'Orchestre* dates from this period, as does a revision of the *Florida* suite, and a first String Quartet.

To GRIEG *Last Saturday Arvesen, a violinist, and Soot, a Norwegian painter, came to me at Ville d'Avray. We played your C minor sonata together, which brought back many memories.*

Ville d'Avray: Corot's lake.

I have been in Ville d'Avray for a week, 35 minutes by train from Paris. I have rented a small 2-roomed cottage, it stands quite alone on the bank of a small lake in the woods. So I am at work again. Close by there is a small restaurant where I eat. It really is lovely here, not a soul and all around, woods and hills. One would think oneself a hundred miles from Paris.

EDVARD GRIEG
And you have written a string quartet! What a wonderful time is this time of youth, when it just pours out of one's heart in one long stream!

From the MS of the early String Quartet.

Portrait of the violinist Arve Arvesen, by Edvard Munch.

In October 1889 came a move to another quiet part of the Parisian *banlieue*—Croissy-sur-Seine—where Delius took an apartment.

No. 8, Boulevard de la Mairie, Croissy.

To GRIEG *I have a suggestion to make: Come here at the beginning of May, then we will also see the World Exhibition.*

An autumn visit to the *Exposition Universelle* (random musical phrases are in fact pencilled on the back of Delius's programme of the Javanese exhibit).

Works composed at Croissy during the period 1889–91 were mostly on a smaller scale—songs and instrumental pieces—but the opera *Irmelin* was begun, *Sleigh Ride* was completed, and a concert overture, *Paa Vidderne*, was given at Christiania (Oslo) in the autumn of 1891—the first public performance of an orchestral work by Delius.

Fritz Delius: Two early sketches by Edvard Munch, and a first evidence of their friendship.

Bjørnstjerne Bjørnson.

A summer tour of Norway, which included a visit to Bjørnson, was much prolonged so that he could attend the première of *Paa Vidderne.*

To GRIEG, from Fredriksvaern
I arrived here yesterday from Aulestad where I spent a week with Bjørnson in a very pleasant way . . . I am staying a fairly long time in Norway this year in order to hear my overture, which Holter is going to perform.

GRIEG to BJØRNSON
I have just got one of your guests in my home.—The Englishman Delius, a talented modern musician—an idealist by nature. I am going to the Jotunheim with him . . .

CHRISTIAN SINDING
I have always admired you for so well understanding how to keep to your main plan and not let yourself be influenced too much by external circumstances.

Warmuths Kgl. Hof-Musikhandel og Concertbureau.

Musikforeningens
1ste Concert
Lørdag den 10de Oktober 1891 Kl. 8
i Tivolis Cirkuslokale
under Ledelse af
Hr. Iver Holter
og under Medvirkning af
**Hr. Violinist Fred. Frederiksen og
Hr. Barytonsanger Salomon Smith.**

Program.

1. **Holter, Iver:** Suite for stort Orkester efter Musikken til „Götz v. Berlichingen".
   a. Hyldningsmarsch.
   b. Stilleben, Menuet i gammel Stil.
   c. Scene i Skoven.
   d. Erotik.
   e. Vehmgericht.
   f. Festligt Optog.
   } Manuskript 1ste Gang.

2. **Raff, Joach.:** Concert for Violin med Orkester (1ste Sats).
   Hr. Fredrik Frederiksen.

3. **Wagner, Rich.:** Wotans Abschied und Feuerzauber for Baryton med Orkester (1ste Gang). Hr. Salomon Smith.

4. a. **Wagner,-Wilhelmj:** Romanze med Orkester.
   b. **Popper, David:** Elfentanz med Orkester.
   Hr. Fredrik Frederiksen.

5. a. **Sjögren, Emil:** Bergmanden.
   b. **Elling, Cath.:** Jeg vil ud. Hr. Salomon Smith.

6. **Delius, Fritz:** „Paa Vidderne". Concertouverture for stort Orkester. (1ste Gang) Manuskript.
   Accompagnatør: Hr. Albert Riefling.

Piano fra Warmuth's Pianolager.

On his return to Paris in October Delius moved again—this time to a small apartment at no. 33 rue Ducouëdic, in the Petit Montrouge quarter.

His circle widened: a growing preoccupation with opera saw him briefly in London early in 1892 enlisting the help of the English poet Richard Le Gallienne. Although their joint project did not materialize, Delius's work on *Irmelin* continued.

Richard and Mildred Le Gallienne at their home in Hanwell, Middlesex.

RICHARD LE GALLIENNE
We liked him much. He is sure to do something. I never saw a man with such irresistible will, and as it is directed with intelligence, he is sure to come to the front. Certainly he deserves to. We have sketched out the plot of a little opera together on the story of Endymion—and he has gone back full of it. He seems to have the working capacities of a brewer's horse. Would they were mine!

A friendship begun in the early nineties was with the painter, Daniel de Monfreid.

WILLIAM MOLARD
Our friend Daniel . . . is a man of talent, an artist by nature, susceptible to influence and spontaneous.

Portrait of Fritz Delius, by Daniel de Monfreid.

JELKA DELIUS
I am very fond of it. The hands and the whole pose was very like him at the time. It is painted by Daniel de Monfreid, the friend of Gauguin.

Isidore de Lara.

Making the acquaintance in Paris of another Englishman, the composer Isidore de Lara, Delius came more often into contact with Parisian high society.

A new, if passing, interest—occultism—showed him in a fresh light as caster of horoscopes.

ISIDORE DE LARA
The Princesse Brancaccia is in a great state of anxiety about her horoscope. She is coming here today at 2, could you come and meet her . . .

It was an introduction by de Lara to Princess Alice of Monaco which secured for Delius an orchestral performance—in the Principality—of the reworked *Paa Vidderne*, **last heard in an earlier form in Christiania.**

Princess Alice of Monaco.

PRINCESS ALICE OF MONACO
Let me tell you how fine I thought your 'Sur les Cimes' yesterday. It is splendid music, very highly pushed—and I would be very much surprised if you don't attain 'Les Cimes' of glory—for you have great science coupled to great art. . . .

LE FIGARO, 2 March 1894
The seventh international concert of the season was devoted to English works. A rich programme, including . . . a symphonic poem, *Sur les cimes* (1st performance), by Delius, which was particularly noticed by true musicians and in which the orchestra of M. Steck wrought wonders.

DELIUS ET PAPUS
"

ANATOMIE & PHYSIOLOGIE

DE

L'ORCHESTRE

AVEC UNE PLANCHE ET NOMBREUX TABLEAUX

Prix : Un franc

PARIS

CHAMUEL, ÉDITEUR

29, RUE DE TRÉVISE, 29

1894

Title-page of *Anatomie*.

'Papus', Dr Gérard Encausse.

An introduction to one of Paris's contemporary giants in the occult sciences gave birth to an unusual collaboration and a rather obscure booklet.

Letters from the composer Ottokar Nováček, a fellow student from Leipzig days, bring bemused thanks for the book, and a caricature of Christian Sinding.

OTTOKAR NOVÁČEK
Thank you for your Anatomy and Physiology of the Orch;—I was not able to translate everything, but I personally feel myself to be a stranger to your views.—
How is your opera going? Give my kind regards to Sinding . . .

CHRISTIAN SINDING
How are you getting on with palmistry and astrology? And your pyramidal studies?

By the mid-nineties Delius had become an active member of the circle round an amateur composer, William Molard, who together with his wife held open house for artist friends who cared to call at their studio in the rue Vercingétorix.

I met Strindberg at the studio of Ida Ericson, a Swedish sculptress married to William Molard, a Franco-Norwegian composer. Later on I saw him quite frequently at the crémerie of the Mère Charlotte, in the Rue de la Grande Chaumière (Montparnasse) where artists received unlimited credit.

Madame Charlotte Caron at the window above her crémerie, no. 13 rue de la Grande Chaumière.

William Molard at work on a score in Gauguin's studio.

Far right:
Portrait of Gauguin, by Judith Ericson-Molard.

Among the habitués of the Mère Charlotte at that time were Strindberg, Gauguin, Mucha, a Czech designer of decorations and affiches, Leclercq, a poet, a Polish painter named Slewinski, the maître de ballet *from the Folies-Bergères—also a Czech—and myself. I lived at Montrouge and generally took my meals at home, but I occasionally lunched or dined at the* crémerie *to meet Gauguin and Strindberg. Or I would sometimes fetch Strindberg for a walk in the afternoon . . .*

ALPHONSE MUCHA

. . . in addition to being our eating place, Madame Charlotte's crémerie also served as a sort of private academy where everybody explained his work and tried to win over the others to his opinions.

The courtyard of no. 6 rue Vercingétorix, in Montparnasse, with the Molards' studio (centre, below) and above it that of Gauguin.

Opera continued to preoccupy Delius, and the composition of the exotic *Magic Fountain* dates from this period. Even so, there can be no doubt that he was to an extent diverted from the main task of composition as he moved in and out of this kaleidoscopic group of artists, writers and musicians. Inevitably his horizons were widened and his artistic tastes developed and sharpened.

Among the students at the Académie Colarossi, also in the rue de la Grande Chaumière, was a young German painter, Ida Gerhardi. Her closest friend and fellow student was another young artist, from Schleswig-Holstein, Jelka Rosen.

Jelka Rosen, centre, kneeling, and Ida Gerhardi, right.

The Bohemian soirées at the studios of Gauguin and the Molards have become legendary. Delius was often among the guests.

JUDITH ERICSON-MOLARD

[Gauguin] did not bear the mark of sordid poverty that was on all the artists of our milieu, both those who have succeeded since those days and those who hung fire (with the exception of Frederic Delius, who, obviously, is rich). But Gauguin bubbles over with an inner richness, he is the MASTER overshadowing all the others, even Delius, all reduced to figuring as zeros behind this absolute figure.

Ida Molard in her studio.

There is a man named Leclercq who I don't care for much . . .

Julien Leclercq.

ERNEST DOWSON to AUBREY BEARDSLEY

[He] looks as if he had just stepped out of one of your pictures.

At the rue Vercingétorix: a group of friends in Gauguin's studio, including Sérusier (standing, left) and Gauguin's mistress Annah 'la Javanaise'.

28

Slewinski with Bunch of Flowers, by Paul Gauguin.

Nevermore, by Paul Gauguin.

Edvard Munch: Self-portrait with cigarette.

I should . . . like to give all my works a deeper meaning. I want to say something to the world very serious and music and poetry are only my means . . . I want to tread in Wagner's footsteps and even give something more in the right direction. For me dramatic art is almost taking the place of religion. People are sick of being preached to. But by being played to, they may be worked upon.

I have a vague idea of writing 3 works: One on the Indians, one on the Gypsies and one on the Negroes and quadroons. The Indians I am doing at present.

Delius probably met Florent Schmitt in the context of the Molard circle. The young French composer was to make piano transcriptions of four of his friend's operas: *Irmelin, The Magic Fountain, Koanga* **and** *A Village Romeo and Juliet.*

Florent Schmitt.

LÉON MOREAU
Schmitt is busy working on your reduction.

An extract from Schmitt's vocal score of *The Magic Fountain.*

CHRISTIAN SINDING
I was most impressed to hear that you have already completed a new opera . . . I admire your energy in forging ahead so ceaselessly in spite of family and uncles. Eventually you are bound to have a lucky break.

Portrait of August Strindberg, by Edvard Munch.

The acquaintance with Strindberg in Paris dates from around the end of 1894, but there is no evidence that Delius ever turned to the Swedish writer's work for inspiration. A deepening of his musical language is remarked, however, in his settings of some Verlaine poems the following year—among the very few French settings he made.

THOMAS BEECHAM
. . . his growing power to give utterance to moments of dramatic intensity in the second of the two Verlaine songs . . . with its powerful and unexpected climax in the setting of the words 'Qu'as-tu fait de ta jeunesse'. Rarely I think can a lament over lost happiness in youth have been sung more poignantly.

ALPHONSE MUCHA, on Strindberg at the crémerie. He was a remarkable person in every respect—tall and slim, with an enterprising moustache on his upper lip, always well dressed. Every day he would sit in the corner near the bar with a cigarette in his mouth, amusing both himself and us with his ready answers. But he was not a cheerful man. He rarely laughed.

From the MS of the Verlaine song: *Le ciel est, par-dessus le toit.*

From Strindberg's copy of the photograph of Paul Verlaine on his death-bed.

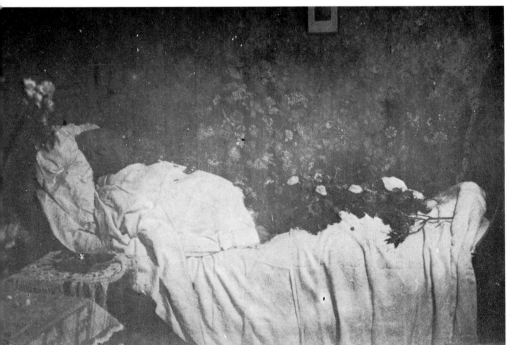

Shortly after Paul Verlaine had died, Strindberg showed me a large photograph of the poet on his death-bed and asked me what I saw on it. I answered candidly that I saw Verlaine lying on his back, under a rather thick eiderdown, only his head and beard being visible; and a pillow that had fallen on the floor and was lying there rather crunched up. Strindberg, however, asked me, did I not see the huge animal lying on Verlaine's stomach and the imp crouching on the floor?

The closest of Delius's Parisian friendships was with Edvard Munch. Innocently, he and Munch precipitated one of the most serious of Strindberg's nervous crises.

Edvard Munch: Self-portrait with skeleton arm.

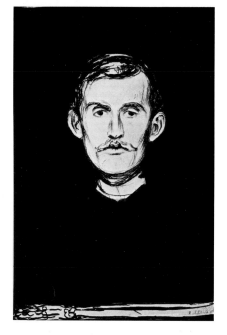

I don't see many Norwegians here apart from Munck—

Strindberg . . . was also occupied with alchemy at that time and claimed to have extracted gold from earth which he had collected in the Cimetière Montparnasse. He showed me pebbles entirely coated with the precious metal and asked me to have one of these samples analysed by an eminent chemist of my acquaintance. My friend examined it and found it to be covered with pure gold. He was hugely interested . . .

He was constantly imagining that attempts were being made to assassinate him by occult or other means. On one occasion Edvard Munch . . . and I called on him at his rooms in the Rue d'Assas. He was poring over his retorts, stirring strange and evil-smelling liquids, and after chatting for five or ten minutes we left him in a most friendly manner. Next day Munch received a post card from him.

STRINDBERG to MUNCH, 19 July 1896
The gas apparatus seems to be based on Pettenkofer's experiment: blow out a light through a wall. But it works badly. Last time I saw you I thought you looked like a murderer—or at least his accomplice.

Strindberg immediately abandoned his apartment and went into hiding elsewhere in Paris. Within a fortnight he had fled to Sweden, and Delius was never to see him again.

Chemical analysis made on Strindberg's behalf, sent to the Princesse de Cystria, and ultimately retained by Delius.

Jelka Rosen, by Ida Gerhardi.

Jelka Rosen met and fell in love with Delius early in 1896.

The first letter to JELKA ROSEN, 1 March 1896
Dear Miss Rosen
   I thank you very much for your kind note and will, as you propose, come on Monday night. . . . Your sympathetic words about my music gave me great pleasure . . .

Jelka introduced Delius to the village of Grez-sur-Loing, where she painted in the summer months.

A place like this one could really work in; everything is quiet and unspoilt.

Your description of Grez really makes one long to be there; I must spend a summer there once or perhaps I might spend this autumn there! The old garden certainly must look beautiful . . . are you painting something new?

ROBERT LOUIS STEVENSON
A low bridge of many arches choked with sedge; great fields of white and yellow water-lilies; poplars and willows innumerable . . .

AUGUST STRINDBERG
The village is situated where the plateau slopes down to the river Loing (tributary of the Seine). Standing outside the village on the highway and looking towards the white cluster of houses one immediately recognises the archetypal French village, mother of the city, or city in miniature. It is surrounded by windowless walls. The village is blind. Is it the window-tax or defence that has fashioned these long stretches of walls? Perhaps both. It is white, but has black roofs, of blackened tiles. It is happy, but sad at the same time. The village is said to be an invention of the Romans, the garden an invention of the Teutons. . . . Looking into the village one can see two rows of single-storeyed houses flanking the main street which lies cobbled in between. There are gutters on either side of the cobblestones, but there is no paving in front of the houses. Ducks paddle in the gutters and chickens promenade in the street. The first house that comes to notice is the buvette or tavern. For its signboard it has a juniper bush sticking out. Next comes the baker's sign, then the tobacconist's shield with its government number, for tobacco is a monopoly, as is well known. Further away, the hotel, where commercial travellers and tourists can find a bed. On a bend in the street stand the ruins of the old castle under whose protection these peasants once settled, but whose name and owner have been forgotten. It would seem from its arches and ornamentation to date from the 13th century. Then come the butcher's, the general store, the church. Beyond the latter are the presbytery, the mairie and the school.

It was in 1896 that a set of songs—some new, some retranslated—was issued: his first publication in Paris.

5 Chansons

Berceuse	4
La ballade du musicien	5
Chant Indien	6
Plus vite mon cheval	5
Il pleure dans mon cœur	4

Musique
de

FRITZ DELIUS

PARIS
L. GRUS FILS, Éditeur, 116, B^d Haussmann

Delius had other women friends—notably the Princesse de Cystria (to whom he had dedicated one edition of his song *Plus vite, mon cheval*) and, on a more platonic note, Mrs. Jutta Bell, whom he had first come to know as a neighbour in Florida and who was now helping him with the plot and libretto of his latest opera, *Koanga*.

Before long the libretto was entrusted to a professional writer, C. F. Keary, an Englishman living near Grez.

Jutta Bell.

An extract from Keary's original libretto for *Koanga*.

From MS sketches for *Koanga*.

The opera's hero, Koanga, is based on the African slave-prince Bras-Coupé in G. W. Cable's novel *The Grandissimes*.

I am writing another opéra—Please keep this quite to yourself—I am taking the story of Bras-Coupé—in The Grandissimes—Read it and tell me what you think of it—I will send you shortly the libretto and no doubt you will be able to give me some help. I am getting all the Southern flavor in the music.

I dont believe in realism in opéra—Fantasy and poetry . . . I am employing the Banjo in my orchester. The effect will be strange—

At present all goes well. I am working on a work which I believe will be unique in its way . . . I must not tell you but my money matters are just as bad as ever, nay! even worse. I cannot sell a song; It seems ridiculous when one comes to think of it but I cannot make a fiver—

Bras-Coupé (Koanga), by Alfred Herter.

There are many curious links in Delius's Scandinavian-flavoured works. Jens Peter Jacobsen's verses were used by the composer in six of his *Seven Danish Songs*. This portrait of Jacobsen was painted by the Swedish artist Ernst Josephson, who was also a poet of distinction and whose *Black Roses* furnished Delius with his only Swedish source-work.

I have written 5 songs to J. P. Jacobsen's poems—I think they are good. However I cannot find a publisher who will pay me and I am not going to publish anything more gratis, even if I die of starvation.

Review by CLAUDE DEBUSSY in *LA REVUE BLANCHE*, 1 April 1901
Je ne vois guère à retenir après cela que des 'Poèmes Danois' pour chant et orchestre de Fritz Delius: ce sont des chansons très douces, très blanches, de la musique pour bercer les convalescentes dans les quartiers riches . . . Il y a toujours une note qui se traîne sur un accord; telle, sur un lac, une fleur de nénuphar fatiguée d'être regardée par la lune, ou bien encore . . . un petit aérostat bloqué par les nuages. C'était ineffable comme tout, cette musique!

Right: From the MS of *Black Roses*.
Below: From the MS full score of the *Seven Danish Songs*: a setting of Jacobsen's *Det bødes der for.*

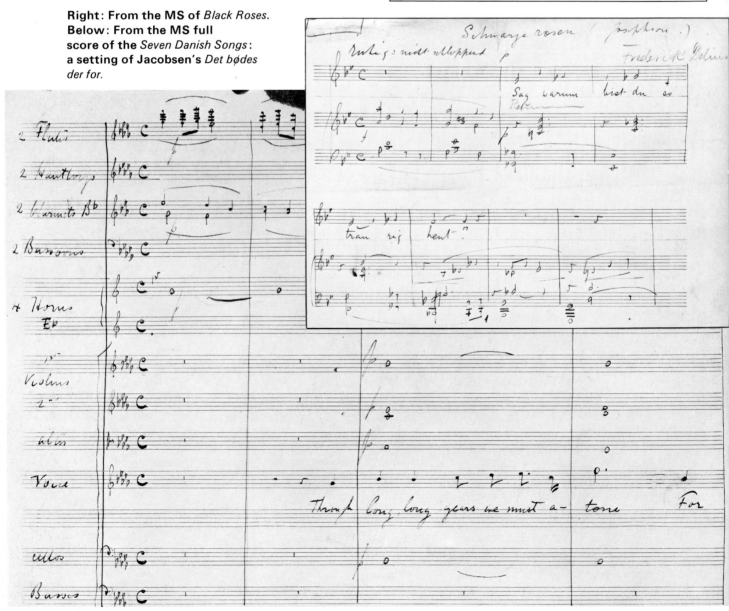

Early in 1897 Delius revisited America, anxious to find a means of turning his abandoned orange farm to useful account. He looked up old friends in Danville and Jacksonville and while at Solana Grove worked on his piano concerto.

Returning in the summer he made his way to Grez-sur-Loing, where Jelka and her mother had bought a house which they now shared for a while with Ida Gerhardi.

Ida Gerhardi: Self-portrait.

IDA GERHARDI

Although I speak without any real authority, Delius has found a wonderful perfection in his compositions here in Grez. He himself says things haven't gone like this before—the tranquillity, the poetry of the landscape and at the same time the constant stimulus which he has through Jelka and me being near him give him one fresh idea after another . . . he is an artist through and through, refined and nervous temperamentally.

Grez: View from the bridge.

The Norwegian dramatist, Gunnar Heiberg, visited Delius in Grez and asked him to write incidental music to his play *Folkeraadet* (The People's Parliament). Delius went to Christiania in October 1897 for the première which was marked by stormy scenes, largely on account of what was considered to be the composer's parody of the Norwegian national anthem.

Gunnar Heiberg, by Edvard Munch.

No one speaks any more of Heiberg's piece, now it is only my music. Chr[ist]iania is divided into two camps—for or against—all the good artists are for. All the bourgeois are against. I have been with Ibsen quite a good deal and he was delighted and congratulated me most heartily. Every night in the theatre there is a pitched battle when the music begins. Hissing and hurrahs. There was some talk about lynching me . . .

Henrik Ibsen at the Café of the Grand Hotel, Christiania, by Edvard Munch.

In Norway the composer now became a controversial public figure. Christian Krohg, a leading painter (and teacher of Munch), came to sketch and interview him for *Verdens Gang*, a daily newspaper.

NEWSPAPER INTERVIEW, CHRISTIANIA, OCTOBER 1897

. . . Are you working on anything else now?

Yes, two operas. One on a Red Indian theme and the other a fairy-tale.

Red Indian? Yes, of course, you own a plantation in America.

Yes, but it is in Florida. There aren't any Indians there. Only negroes.

What do you grow there?

Tobacco and oranges. Excellent tobacco. Would you care to try one from my plantation? You're very welcome.

He produced an extremely fine Havana cigar.

Do you spend much time on your plantation?

No. I was there last winter and had the young Norwegian composer Jebe with me. It's nice in the winter, not too hot. Jasmine grows wild in all the forests in January.

Would you care to sell your plantation, Mr Delius? said a well-known Christiania lawyer, who was sitting next to him.

Yes. Would you care to buy it?

I should like to have a plantation. Come round to my office tomorrow.

Delius got up to go . . .

The Christiania Theatre.

WILLIAM MOLARD to EDVARD MUNCH

Delius . . . has certainly had a real success in Norway and has kept the newspapers rather busy; this has been fortunate for him, because at any rate attention has now been drawn to Delius's name up there and this can never do any harm.

Delius then travelled from Norway to Elberfeld in order to be present at the first performance of a work of his in Germany: *Over the Hills and Far Away*. Ida Gerhardi had effected his introduction to the conductor Hans Haym, who was to be the first effective champion of his music.

TÄGLICHER ANZEIGER, Elberfeld, 16 November 1897
The opening evoked interest and tension, and the work is certainly rich in original ideas and pretty melodies and is in many places brilliantly and skilfully scored. But it did not hang together logically, and generally lacked a clear train of thought. Furthermore, the colours were often laid on too crudely.

Ferruccio Busoni, whom he had known since Leipzig days, was in Paris the following January and was showing interest in the recently-completed Piano Concerto.

I am spending a lot of time with Busoni who is playing my concerto with me tomorrow à deux pianos. He may help me considerably as he likes my music.

Hans Haym.

From an autograph MS of the solo part of the Piano Concerto.

Ferruccio Busoni.

One of Delius's many female Norwegian admirers was the pianist, Charlotte Bødtker Naeser. She sent him a coquettish note from Chile, together with her photograph.

CHARLOTTE BØDTKER NAESER
I send you this picture not because it is a good one, or very much like the original . . . But I have my own reasons for sending it: I don't think any gentleman who did not want to be very rude could do anything else than return his own photo . . .
I hope you won't disappoint me. I am very often thinking about you, and you would make me feel very happy.

Daniel de Monfreid: Self portrait.

Later in 1898 it was in the company of another Norwegian woman that he called on Daniel de Monfreid, with a view to buying one of the Gauguin pictures held by de Monfreid. Theodor Delius had recently died and this was the first use to which his nephew put a part of his legacy.

DANIEL DE MONFREID, *Diaries*
Tuesday 8 November 1898 . . . Delius comes with a Norwegian lady. He buys Gauguin's femme couchée (Never more) and I go with him to a picture framer's.

DANIEL DE MONFREID, *Diaries*
Friday 11 November 1898 At 11 o'clock Delius visits me and brings 500 fr. for Gauguin price of the picture he has bought. After lunch I write to Gauguin.

PAUL GAUGUIN to DANIEL DE MONFREID
You did well to let Delius have the picture 'Nevermore' . . . I'm very glad Delius is its owner, seeing that it isn't a speculative purchase for resale, but bought because he likes it; then some other time he'll want another, especially if callers compliment him on it or get him to talk about the subject.

Nevermore, by Paul Gauguin.

DANIEL DE MONFREID to PAUL GAUGUIN
I am glad you don't disapprove of the sale to Delius. As a matter of fact he's a lad who likes your painting, and especially this canvas. Not because of the title; he told me that himself. But because it is a *beautiful painting*.

As with Gauguin, Delius's Paris years left another kind of legacy: he contracted syphilis.

By far the larger part of his uncle's legacy was devoted to financing a major concert of Delius's compositions in London in May 1899. Armed with introductions from Fauré, Delius set out full of hope for London.

Gabriel Fauré and a few of the best young French musicians played my opera at Mrs. Maddison's this afternoon. Prince and Princess de Polignac and a few other musical people were there and I think I may say they were quite enthusiastic. It gives me a little more confidence for London.

Gabriel Fauré, by John Singer Sargent.

Letter of introduction from Gabriel Fauré to Lady Lewis.

John Singer Sargent, by William Rothenstein.

The concert, conducted by Alfred Hertz, was to represent a review of all the best that he had composed up till that time. Fauré's London friends helped to stir up interest in musical circles.

JOHN SINGER SARGENT

Lady Lewis has allowed me to be associated with her in a plan to become acquainted with some of your works before the Concert—and to have our friends hear them at her home.

JOHN SINGER SARGENT

It is very kind of you to let me come to a rehearsal and I have marked down that of the 29th at 2.30 . . . I am absolutely prevented from going to your Concert, which I feel to be a very great calamity to myself—

London's West End at the turn of the century.

I don't hope for any success whatever. It takes the English people too long to get accustomed to anything.

A concert was given at St. James's Hall, this evening, which proved to be of quite exceptional interest. It was organised by Mr. Fritz Delius (a native of Yorkshire, but of Scandinavian parentage, and trained abroad), the programme consisting entirely of his compositions. It may be said at once that Mr. Delius is a composer of powerful individuality and independence, with a great deal to say and a striking way of saying it. He has the rarest of all powers—that of at once making the hearer realise what he wants to convey. By means of harmony as well as by orchestral colouring, he creates an "atmosphere" at will, and whether in songs, in symphonic poems, or in opera, he always arrests attention by legitimate means, and knows how to retain it. He has an astonishing power of inventing new orchestral effects, but they subserve his main purpose, and are not dragged in for their own sake. We ought to hear much more of Mr. Delius.

Manchester Courier, **31 May 1899.**

The Concert of course has done me an immense amount of good and has placed me amongst the first composers of today—The German papers also have long articles.

EDVARD MUNCH
Your success in London pleased me very much and I congratulate you from the bottom of my heart.—

PROGRAMME.

ALL COMPOSITIONS BY FRITZ DELIUS.

PART I.

1 FANTASIA, "Over the Hills and Far Away" (for Orchestra).

2 LÉGENDE, for Violin and Orchestra.
   *Solo Violin—*MR. JOHN DUNN.

3 SUITE, for Orchestra (composed for the satiric drama, "The Council of the People," by Gunnar Heiberg).
   3rd and 4th Movements.

4 DANISH SONGS (with Orchestral Accompaniment).
   (a) "Through long, long Years."
   (b) "Let Springtime come, then."
   (c) "Irmelin Rose."
   (d) "On the Seashore."
   (e) "Wine Roses."
   MDLLE. CHRISTIANNE ANDRAY.

5 SYMPHONIC POEM, "The Dance goes on" (for Orchestra).

6 "MITTERNACHTS LIED" from "Also Sprach Zarathustra."
   (Friedrich Nietzsche)
   Baritone Solo, Men's Chorus, and Orchestra.
   *Vocalist—*MR. DOUGLAS POWELL.

PART II.

EXCERPTS FROM "KOANGA"—Opera in three acts, with a prologue and epilogue (libretto by C. F. Keary, taken from the Novel by George W. Cable, "The Grandissimes.")

1 - - - (a) Prelude to Act III.
         (b) Quintet and Finale of Act I.
2 - - - Act II.

Vocalists.
MME. ELLA RUSSELL, MISS TILLY KOENEN,
MR. G. A. VANDERBEECK, MR. WM. LLEWELLYN,
AND MR. ANDREW BLACK.

MRS. ADEY BRUNEL
Delius fought against having his photograph taken. At last he consented and I took him to Window & Grove. He half laughed and half swore under his breath all the time—'See what a fool you are making of me!' 'I feel such a damned fool!'—But at lunch afterwards he quite forgave me and said I *was* right; though the photographs are not to be given out to any paper that asked for them.

Despite the interest shown on all sides in the highly original music included in this ambitious programme, his own parents still refused to acknowledge the gifts of their son . . .

JULIUS DELIUS's only comment on the day after the events:
I see Fritz has given a concert.

MRS. JULIUS DELIUS
. . . more money for you is quite out of the question. Go to America or remain it is the same to us. We shall be pleased if you become famous and hope so, but *we* have done our share towards it and *nobody* can say that we have not . . . My belief is that Paris has spoiled you altogether.

. . . and publishers were slow to see any notably marketable qualities in his compositions.

I saw Hansen today and mentioned my songs but he did not seem anxious to publish them, said he had so many things in hand so of course I let the subject drop. I really am no good vis à vis editors and am sure only make an indifferent or bad impression . . . I shall let the matter drop and send my music [to Schott, in Mainz] after I have written—as I have just had my hair cut very short—it was so hot—my chances are still less. I think on the whole Verleger had better not see me as I have 'nichts Geniales' in my appearance.

Andrew Black—the first Koanga.

Paris.

The completion of the 'Nocturne' *Paris (the Song of a Great City)* **shortly after the London concert marked the close of the long years of apprenticeship.**

JULIUS BUTHS
In parts I find the piece quite outstanding, as outstanding as anything anywhere in music, but this absolute non-acknowledgement of rules and laws —.

Sketches for *Paris.*

Two years passed before Haym was able to take the work into his repertoire and to give the first performance.

TÄGLICHER ANZEIGER, Elberfeld, 15 December 1901
If only all the bizarre had been omitted and there remained just the elegiac passages full of expressive melody and the poetical ending, then we would indeed have a tone poem which truly reflects the unforgettable impression that we receive at night alone in front of the Sacré Coeur. However the composer takes us by the arm, sits us on an omnibus and dashes with us from one cabaret to another.

Jelka Rosen in 1897 by Ida Gerhardi

Jelka Rosen in 1901 by Ida Gerhardi

Delius in 1903, by Ida Gerhardi

The Garden at Grez, by Jelka.

Maturity, 1900–14

The composition of *Paris* may be seen as a symbolic farewell to the city. Delius retained an apartment there for some years but he was now settled at Grez with Jelka. Among the friends they entertained during these early years at Grez was the sculptor Auguste Rodin.

JELKA ROSEN to RODIN
The lilacs are in bud—will they bring you here?
Can I tempt you by telling you that there is a *very* artistic musician here who is a fervent admirer of your art, a great enthusiast of your Balzac, who would be *very* very happy to make your acquaintance?

AUGUSTE RODIN to JELKA ROSEN
You give generously to me of your soul and from it I take much joy. Yes, I shall come to see you. I must escape and just as soon as I possibly can.

JELKA ROSEN to RODIN
I think of our fresh morning walk last summer as of something heavenly and impossibly far away. Then I see your superb profile against my intimate and beloved countryside of Grez.

Jelka painting.

ACHILLE OUVRÉ to JELKA ROSEN
. . . the little garden pleases me although the green patch of foliage on the wall is too opaque for the rest.

The first major work of Delius's maturity was the opera *A Village Romeo and Juliet*, written largely at Grez, and based on the novella by Gottfried Keller.

I am sick of losing time over concerts when they are not absolutely necessary for my development. I don't care a d--- for fame of any sort, and would rather be at my work.

When I have done here I should like to settle down and finish R.J.

My second act is done . . .

From letters to Jelka when Delius was in Berlin, January–March 1901.

From Florent Schmitt's vocal score of *A Village Romeo and Juliet*; the voice parts and English words are in Delius's hand.

For all the influence of
established figures like Fauré and
Messager and the help of
younger friends like Florent
Schmitt and Ravel, Delius's music
had made no impression on Paris,
and his French friends were
gradually ceding ground to his
new protagonists in Germany.
Soon he was to enjoy a vogue
rivalling that for the mighty
Strauss.

Richard Strauss.

Paris began to arouse interest in Germany. If Strauss's initial reaction
on perusing the score was negative, a year later in 1903 he took a more
favourable view. Julius Buths, conductor in Düsseldorf, made a version
for two pianos, and Busoni directed a full orchestral performance in
Berlin in 1902.

RICHARD STRAUSS

I have read your score: Paris with great interest! I am afraid I cannot
decide to perform the work for the time being: the symphonic development
seems to me to be too scant, and it seems moreover to be an imitation of
Charpentier which has not quite succeeded—perhaps I cannot quite
imagine the effect of the piece, and I beg you kindly to forgive me and in
any case not to be discouraged if, with regret, I return your score to you
unperformed.

JULIUS BUTHS

'Paris' for two pianos is finished; I am now having a copy made so that I
can play the piece shortly with Dr. Haym. Friend Haym is doing the same
with your 'Lebenstanz' and I am very much looking forward to getting to
know it.

JULIUS BUTHS

Last Friday we played your two works 'Paris' and 'Lebenstanz' to Strauss
in Cologne. The impression they made on Strauss was definitely in your
favour.

From Ravel's vocal score of *Margot la Rouge*. **Delius has completed the bars left blank by Ravel.**

Delius had probably met Maurice Ravel at the Molards' studio in the late nineties. In 1902 he asked him to undertake a piano transcription of a one-act opera, *Margot la Rouge*, which was subsequently entered — without success — for the Sonzogno Prize.

MAURICE RAVEL

The transcription is well under way but I must ask you to give me until the end of this month to finish it; I hope however to be able to send it to you before then.

MAURICE RAVEL

I have transcribed literally certain doubtful passages and will discuss these with you later, except for a few bars (Scene V. *Pourquoi me confier ces choses-là*) which seemed mysterious to me, and which I have left blank. I would also draw your attention to one line without music in the orchestral score (Scene II *La Patronne: Il te pince donc bien, ton nouveau béguin*).

Maurice Ravel, by Achille Ouvré.

In March 1903 Edvard Munch came to stay for a time at Grez— the distance from Paris being an added attraction.

EDVARD MUNCH to KAREN BJØLSTAD
I am going to stay outside Paris at Delius's and will keep myself hidden for understandable reasons—

EDVARD MUNCH
I should like to stay a while at your home—it must be very beautiful but I am afraid of a woman in Paris and expect further bad things . . .

JELKA ROSEN to RODIN
Young Munk, a very, very interesting Norwegian painter is here . . .

Two years later
EDVARD MUNCH
Please tell me how Miss Eva Mudocci is—have you seen her?

Miss Eva Mudocci is in Paris, I know, but I have not seen her for a long time. She is very charming.

EVA MUDOCCI to EDVARD MUNCH
You asked about Delius—yes—we have seen him,—last spring he visited us together with his wife, and a few weeks ago they were here again—I like her very much—she is so calm and good-natured and shrewd in a way— she has a good heart too, I feel—he is the same as ever; a little older—a little more Mephistophelian!—they have invited us to their home several times, but we haven't yet been—We played a piece of his music for him— which was a great strain for us because it was so dreadfully boring and we had to look as if we found it interesting! no!—that sounds too spiteful of me!—I like him too—but not his music.

The Violin Concert (Bella Edwards and Eva Mudocci), by Edvard Munch.

The summer of 1903 brought another significant performance—that in Basel of the *Mitternachtslied,* **set from Nietzsche's** *Also sprach Zarathustra.*

I have just come back from Basel where my Mitternachtslied from Zarathustra for baritone solo, male chorus and orchestra was played at the German Tonkünstlerfest—I even think that I have managed to get a publisher thereby!!

TO GRIEG *My 'Mitternachtslied' I don't need to tell you has absolutely no relationship whatever with Strauss's Zarathustra which I consider a complete failure. But I find that 'Till Eulenspiegel' and Heldenleben especially are splendid works. Tod und Verklärung I find not so significant although there is much that is beautiful in it. There is still too much Liszt and Berlioz about it—I think he will do his best work in humorous things. His tragedy is 'Dick und Deutsch'.*

Julius Buths.

If Julius Buths had earlier had reservations about Delius's setting of the *Mitternachtslied* **he had none about** *Appalachia,* **which marked his complete conversion to Delius's music.**

JULIUS BUTHS
Your new work [Appalachia] demonstrates to me that for you everything in the world that you see and experience with emotion can become music, that the world surrounds you in terms of 'sound' and that these sounds you carry in your very being. You 'hear away into distances' into which others have not yet heard; I might say that you lay bare every sinew of sound to our astonished ear.

JULIUS BUTHS
. . . [Delius] the man who has such exceptional confidence in his artistic instinct and his initiative . . .

After sharing a home for six years, Delius and Jelka married in September 1903. With an eye, perhaps, to the possibility of international fame, the narrowly Germanic 'Fritz' was dropped and 'Frederick' adopted.

JELKA ROSEN to RODIN
. . . now we are to be married on the 25th of this month. I am a little apprehensive of this ceremony at the town hall at Grez; but one must no doubt learn to be ridiculous with grace!

TO GRIEG *On the 25th I married my friend Jelka Rosen here in Grez (civilement of course). I have got even further away from God and Jesus. We lived together in 'unrecognized' marriage for 6 years but we found it really more practical to legalize our relationship—one gets everything cheaper and receives gratis and without further ado a certificate of honesty and good morals . . . she is a painter and very gifted . . . I send you and your dear wife my very best wishes and remain, affectionately as ever*
   Yours
   Frederick Delius
   (new name!)

EDVARD GRIEG
You have now reached the zenith of your life, I mean that point in life when the artist does his best work.

The year 1904 signalled the real upsurge of interest in his music in Germany, with *Koanga* receiving its première in Elberfeld in the spring, and four of his works being given in the autumn in two concerts in that same town. His sister Clare came from England to see *Koanga*, which was conducted by Fritz Cassirer.

Fritz Cassirer.

Elberfeld: the Stadttheater.

Elberfeld: the Stadttheater.

From a review of *Koanga* in the *Täglicher Anzeiger*.

CLARE DELIUS

While I was in Elberfeld, Fred took me for walks round the Town, our talk being all of his music. I remember how he conducted me on the pendant tramway over the river—a species of transport called the 'Schwebebahn' which I had never seen anywhere else—and how amused he was at my nervousness, for we seemed suspended by a wheel over the Wupper.

Elberfeld: the Suspension Railway.

Elberfeld.

HANS HAYM
HANS HAYM
He has a more acute ear than the rest of us and because of this he hears and writes down sounds which none before him has heard . . . Delius is a master of the art of lighting upon a mood, portraying it and letting it die away.

JELKA DELIUS to RODIN
. . . this dismal town, full of black smoke, modern industry, machines and rich and very ugly people—

Elberfeld: the Stadthalle, where *Appalachia* (first performance), the Piano Concerto (first performance), *Lebenstanz* and *Paris* were all given during October 1904. Conductor: Hans Haym.

TÄGLICHER ANZEIGER, 18 October 1904
[Appalachia] is not over-extravagant; the compositions of Richard Strauss have seen to it that 'modern' music does not sound too strange to our ears. At various points and wherever, in fact, the bizarre does not gain the upper hand over the musical line, one could enjoy the talent of Herr Delius. But unfortunately the most frequent verdict was 'long-winded'.

TÄGLICHER ANZEIGER, 26 October 1904
Something like a war has been joined here over Delius . . .

AUGUSTE RODIN to JELKA DELIUS
Please convey to Mr. Delius my congratulations on his German successes . . .

On their return from Germany, Jelka visited Rodin in Paris, to be given a long-promised bronze—a smaller version of one of the *Burghers of Calais*. Her involvement with Rodin's art was matched by that of Delius with Munch, who had come to rely heavily on his friend's advice concerning exhibitions and prices in Paris.

Auguste Rodin in his studio, by Ida Gerhardi.

JELKA DELIUS to RODIN

The music of Delius is not the sort that one can like superficially—it is rather like your sculpture—one either finds it abominable, or one loves it with one's whole being.

AUGUSTE RODIN to JELKA DELIUS

I must see you . . . to ask you to accept a keepsake, which you must accept and make me happy. My sculptures have certainly left a mark on your mind, and I shall ask you—which one! I shall have it cast in bronze.

JELKA DELIUS to RODIN

You will never be able to imagine what a joy at all hours your superb bronze is for me—I feel only too deeply that I have not merited it but to love it, to cherish it, to admire it, to understand it better than I—no-one could do this, I feel . . .
The other evening I returned home with my treasure in my arms—in a real fever; my husband is utterly delighted . . .

EDVARD MUNCH

I intend to arrange a fairly large exhibition in Paris in the winter—would you perhaps like to help me—

A performance of *Appalachia* at the Lower Rhine Music Festival in Düsseldorf in May 1905 brought Delius together with some of his main protagonists: *l. to r.* Oskar Fried, Delius, Haym, and Jelka.

Another memorable score, completed in 1903, was published and performed in 1906: *Sea Drift*, to words by Walt Whitman. If its reception by the German musical press was mixed, conductors of standing like Max Schillings and Hans Haym, and of promise like the young Carl Schuricht, had no reservations as to its worth.

Delius.

Review of the first performance of Sea Drift in Essen: *DIE MUSIK*, July 1906

... a work of a depressing despair such as I have scarcely heard before. One continually has the feeling that the composer has composed just off the natural harmony ... What is the good of all the ingenuity that is turned to such a piece if its effect becomes progressively more miserable?

MAX SCHILLINGS

Accept these brief thanks for sending 'Seadrift', the dedication of which is a great and genuine joy to me.

HANS HAYM

Seadrift has made a decided impression and I congratulate you on its success.

Carl Schuricht.

CARL SCHURICHT

Now all this time I could not forget 'Sea-Drift'—whenever I thought of the work my heart beat quicker and I often felt like writing to you about it;—but as long as I had no chorus I was ashamed to keep coming to you with words alone—and not action ... I received [the piano score of 'Sea-Drift'] yesterday by return of post, and I plunged into it with the appetite of a person whose hunger is years old—'yes, yes—, *that's* how it was!' Every note came back to me and, in full draughts, I drank in the tale that I remembered so well from the Essen performance;—I wander around as if intoxicated, what a wonderful gift the piece was and is to me.

Title-page of the vocal score of *Sea Drift.*

From a facsimile of the autograph MS of *Sea Drift.*

The Sun, by Edvard Munch.

FREDERICK DELIUS

EINE MESSE DES LEBENS

FÜR SOLI, CHOR UND
GROSSES ORCHESTER

NACH NIETZSCHES
ZARATHUSTRA
ZUSAMMENGESTELLT
VON FRITZ CASSIRER

Rudolf Haym
6 Elberfeld Katzenberger Str. 220.

KLAVIERAUSZUG MIT DEUTSCHEN
WORTEN VON OTTO SINGER
ENGL. WORTE V. JOHN BERNHOFF.
MK. 16.— NO.
PRICE 8/. NET.

VERLAG HARMONIE,
—BERLIN.—

LONDON: BREITKOPF & HÄRTEL
54 GREAT MARLBOROUGH STR. W.

Title-page of vocal score of
A Mass of Life.

With the composition of *A Mass of Life* in 1904–5 we reach the largest in scale and most ambitious of Delius's works for the concert-hall as opposed to the stage. The work, to passages from Nietzsche's *Zarathustra*, incorporated the earlier setting of the *Mitternachtslied*.

MAX SCHILLINGS
I stand in awe before your gigantic score, whose secrets do not reveal themselves at first glance.

Review of first performance of excerpts from *A Mass of Life* in Munich, June 1908: *DIE MUSIK*, July 1908
. . . Nietzsche's sufficiently well-known attitude to the music of our time would have caused him angrily to dissociate himself from Delius's approach. This aside, one may confidently assert that Delius has much to say that goes beyond the stereotype. He deliberately avoids taking a fixed line in any particular direction, his sounds are there to depict mood and to create atmosphere (a certain affinity to the French School, not least to Debussy, is noticeable), and in this, sustained by clever instrumentation, he often succeeds to perfection, even if his ability to vary expression seems to be rather limited.

HANS HAYM
I thank you for having written this work—I consider it the most significant that has been written since Tristan.

WILLIAM MOLARD
So, you foul pagan cleric, you're a writer of Masses—of life—If ever I write one it will be the Blasphemy of all Blasphemies: *a Black Mass*, the only kind that could tempt a dissolute spirit such as your devoted

Will

I consider Nietzsche the only free thinker of modern times and for me the most sympathetic one—He is at the same time such a poet. He feels Nature. I believe, myself, in no doctrine whatever—and in nothing but in Nature and in the great forces of Nature—

Nietzsche, by Edvard Munch.

From the autograph MS of the *Mitternachtslied Zarathustras.*

In 1907 came the première of *A Village Romeo and Juliet*, which was given in Berlin under Cassirer's baton.

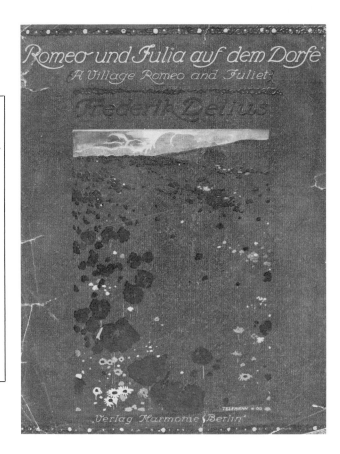

DIE MUSIK, March 1907
He carefully calls his work an Idyll in pictures and indeed simply presents us with mood-paintings; but on the stage we require more, we require clear-cut figures and actions. Add to this the fact that the refined but unfeeling music-making of a Delius is more or less the direct antithesis of Keller's style, and that the vocal line, like the instrumentation, of this despairingly gloomy and confused musical language flouts one's natural feeling for beauty as it flouts all the musical culture we have gained over the centuries. *A Village Romeo and Juliet* is yet another advance for that movement which seeks to derive an advantage from the voguish revaluation of all concepts of musical art . . . It must be said that there was no lack of the usual applause at the première.

Engelbert Humperdinck.

ENGELBERT HUMPERDINCK
'A Village Romeo and Juliet' made an excellent impression on me, particularly the last two acts, which I find most original; as far as the first two acts are concerned I have certain doubts which I would very much like to have discussed with you, but which I think can easily be put right as they are only of a *technical* nature.

Berlin, panorama.

Delius, by Achille Ouvré.

Now firmly established in Germany among the front rank of younger composers and with the satisfaction of having seen his opera given in the capital, Delius left Berlin for another tilt at the London musical establishment. He laid the groundwork during a visit to London in the spring, even if a project to perform *Margot la Rouge* did not succeed.

JOHN COATES

Welcome to England! I have been wanting to get into touch with you for the last 2 or 3 years. Buths of Düsseldorf gave me your address and I lost it. I want to get hold of your songs . . .

Will you come to the annual dinner of our old Bradfordian club at the *New Gaiety tomorrow Friday at 7.30 for 8.* as my guest? Do, it would be delightful. There are not many of us—we are all old Bfd Grammar School boys. You are sure to know all of them—I shall sing a few songs afterwards—

John Coates.

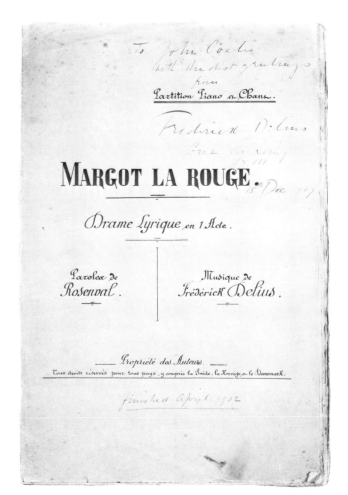

Title-page of printed edition of Ravel's vocal score.

To JOHN COATES *I send you today a one Act music drama 'Margot la Rouge' . . . Perhaps you would translate it. There is a splendid part for you in it. Look it over. My music does not sound well on the piano—so I warn you! But it will be very effective when played.*

It would be worth while to come over here only to see the Turners in the Tate Gallery. Some are quite remarkable and one sees where Monet got his Thames Bridge from. I dined with Balfour Gardiner last night and they played 'Appalachia' through. A few musicians were there. All were tremendously taken with it. This really is my field.

A significant friendship forged during that London spring of 1907 was with Percy Grainger, and it was to Grainger that Delius dedicated his orchestral rhapsody *Brigg Fair*, written later that year. The work was inspired by Grainger's own choral setting of the folk-song.

Percy Grainger.

My star has been most successful and I should have no difficulty here to take the first place. Everybody wants me to come and live in London. I also met Percy Grainger, a most charming young man and more gifted than Scott and less affected . . . He is impulsive and nice.

To GRAINGER *The feeling of nature I think is what I like so much in Grieg's best things. You have it too and I think we all 3 have something in common.*

I consider Percy Grainger the most gifted English composer and the only one who writes English music—and he is an Australian—There is something of the old English robustness and vigor in his music—That part of England which has long ago ceased to exist—or which has emigrated.

PERCY GRAINGER
I never told you of my deep delight at and thankfulness for your dedication of Brigg Fair to me. I had no idea you intended doing so and I am delighted and proud to see my name above that glorious poetic work. I took the score with me to Mengelberg the other day but was glad to hear that he knew it well already. (January 1911)

Sketch for Delius's *Brigg Fair*.

Frederick Delius in 1912, by Jelka Delius

Frederick Delius in 1912, by Ida Gerhardi

Henry Wood had now become interested in Delius's music, effecting in October 1907 its reintroduction to the composer's native land. The revised Piano Concerto in C minor was given at a Promenade Concert, with Théodor Szántó as soloist. In the audience was the young Ralph Vaughan Williams.

ROBIN LEGGE

I did not think the interest sustained to the end, *because* the end was so badly played. But up to 2-3rds—till after the Largo—the poignancy of the emotion was so strong that had you gone on I must have collapsed. I think I never was so moved by modern music as by that . . . for the genuine emotion, for the sheer loveliness of that Largo, I thank you sincerely . . .

Ralph Vaughan Williams.

RALPH VAUGHAN WILLIAMS

I should so much like to show you some of my work. I have had it in my mind (and especially now that I have heard your beautiful concerto) that I should profit very much by your advice and if you saw my work you might be able to suggest ways in which I cd. improve myself—

Henry Wood with The Queen's Hall Orchestra.

Havergal Brian.

Shortly afterwards came a performance of *Appalachia*, conducted by Cassirer at a concert attended by Thomas Beecham. English audiences—and fresh disciples—were now ready for his work.

THOMAS BEECHAM

The first performance in England of *Appalachia* is one of the half-dozen momentous occasions I have known over a period of more than fifty years . . . In a word it was one of the few red-letter days in English music . . .

HAVERGAL BRIAN

I've been going through your 'Appalachia' this morning. It is an extraordinary work, its sincerity makes me weep. I don't know *when* such a surprise offered itself to me.

HAVERGAL BRIAN

There is something noble in your seclusion from the gaping world— working quietly and turning one great thing out on the top of another.

Announcing the first performance in England of *Appalachia*.

CONCERT REVIEW, November 1907
Rarely has a British composer received so cordial a reception as that which was accorded to Mr. Frederick Delius last night at Queen's Hall, after the performance of his Symphonic Poem, *Appalachia*. The audience cheered continually for some minutes in recognition of a British work of the highest merit. When the composer appeared on the platform there was a further demonstration in his honour. It certainly was a memorable scene.

Thomas Beecham.

1908 saw Beecham and Wood preparing performances of major scores. Granville Bantock, too, was to champion his music, and paid a visit to Grez in the summer.

To ETHEL SMYTH [*Beecham*] *is wonderfully gifted and destined to play, perhaps, the most important part in the development of modern music in England. My prophecy! Don't forget it!*

To GRANVILLE BANTOCK *I know there are splendidly musical people in England and also lots of courage and enthusiasm but it is rather thinly spread and suffocated by the others—You see they really love knocking balls about—either kicking them about or knocking them about into holes—and that is devilish bad for music.*

THOMAS BEECHAM

I am trying to arrange for the 'Mass' to be done also in London next season . . . I simply love Sea-Drift—have learnt it by heart and you will be horrified to hear that I play it and sing it on the piano to people up and down the kingdom!!!

Voilà! La résidence de Mohammed.

562 — *Grez-sur-Loing.* - La Grande Rue.

Postcard from Bantock to his wife, 15 July 1908.

HENRY WOOD

Sincerest congratulations upon the great success of your work, 'The Mass of Life' at Munich: I only wish I could have been present . . .
We are working away at 'Sea Drift' for the Sheffield Festival, and the chorus, I think, will sing it splendidly . . . it ought to make a great impression.

THE MUSICAL LEAGUE.
(FOUNDED 1908.)

President.
SIR EDWARD ELGAR.

Vice=President.
FREDERICK DELIUS.

Committee.

PHILIP L. AGNEW.	HARRY EVANS.
IVOR ATKINS.	ARTHUR FAGGE.
GRANVILLE BANTOCK.	ALLEN GILL.
THOMAS BEECHAM.	C. COPELEY HARDING.
A. H. BREWER.	E. HOWARD-JONES.
ADOLPH BRODSKY.	W. G. McNAUGHT.
HAROLD BROOKE.	LANDON RONALD.
H. COWARD.	G. R. SINCLAIR.

HENRY J. WOOD.

Ꜧon. Sec.
NORMAN O'NEILL,
4, Pembroke Villas, Kensington,
London, W.

Assistant=Sec.
W. McNAUGHT, JUNR.,
"Annandale," Woodside Park,
North Finchley, N.

Ꜧon. Treasurer.
J. D. JOHNSTON,
14, Chapel Street, Liverpool.

The founding of The Musical League, with Delius being appointed Vice-President, led to a Festival devoted largely to the works of English composers, in Liverpool in 1909.

From the original opening of *In a Summer Garden:* **autograph MS.**

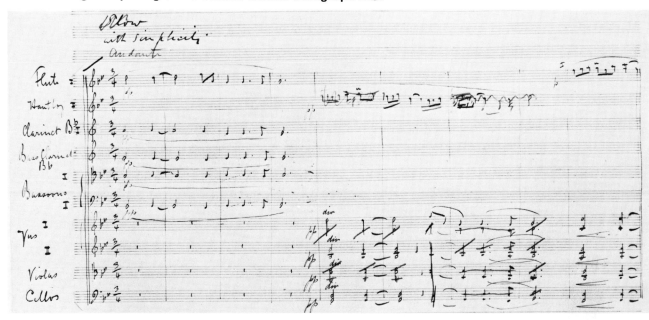

Delius in the garden at Grez, by Jelka.

Having completed yet another choral and orchestral work, *Songs of Sunset*, the previous year, Delius wrote his first *Dance Rhapsody* and the first version of *In a Summer Garden* in 1908. The latter work he dedicated to Jelka and himself conducted the first performance in December that year.

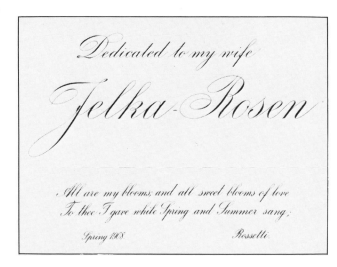

Portrait head of Delius, by Jelka.

Jelka's admiration for Rodin and her absorption of his influence gave us one of the finest likenesses of the composer.

The first performance of *In a Summer Garden.*

I was quite cool when I found myself on the conducting stand and made no mistake. The orchestra played most beautifully and it sounded beautifully for me. I don't believe many people understood the piece but they received it very favourably and called me three times. Busoni wants me to conduct it on Jan 2nd in Berlin but I have not decided yet. What shall I do?

I conducted without a catastrophe and that is about all—I don't think I shall try any more—

And now, a concert review of 1909 gives one of the earliest indications of American interest in Delius's music.

DIE MUSIK, July 1909
Boston: At the Symphony Concert we heard Frederick Delius's symphonic poem 'Paris, a Nocturne'. The music is vague and fragmentary. A little more nocturnal calm would have made a good contrast to the tumult of the crowd.

The first complete *Mass of Life* was given in London by Beecham in June 1909. The work was next performed in Elberfeld in December by Haym, who gave a repeat performance two years later. Two young Hungarians, Béla Bartók and Zoltan Kodály, made their way to yet another performance, in Vienna, in February 1911. Deeply impressed by *Brigg Fair* at the Zürich Festival the previous year, they were now overwhelmed by the *Mass*.

BÉLA BARTÓK, Zürich, 1910
For us the most important impression was meeting Delius.

BÉLA BARTÓK
I am so alone here, have no-one to talk to, apart from my only friend Kodály, and have never met anyone anywhere else to whom, right from the start, I have felt so close as to you. And this is what made my time at the Zürich Festival one of the most beautiful periods of my life.

To assist his young admirers over a copyright question, Delius allowed them the use of his name on their piano pieces published at this time.

ZOLTAN KODÁLY
Our publisher insists that the name of a foreign musician must be printed on the piano pieces he is now issuing, as 'Revisor'. If this is missing (e.g. 'Revised by F. Delius') then the things are copied in America, as Hungary is not yet a member of this International Convention . . .
If another person's name has to appear on our music, then there is hardly any other we would sooner see there than yours.

Kodály and Bartók.

From **Bartók**: *2 Danses Roumaines*
(1910)

From **Kodály**: *10 pièces pour le piano*
(1910)

BÉLA BARTÓK and ZOLTAN KODÁLY
We are about to return home to Budapest from the performance of your 'Mass of Life', which made a deep impression on us.

BÉLA BARTÓK
I can write and tell you what it was that moved me most in the Mass. It was 'der alte Mittag' and 'O Mensch! gieb Acht'. I wonder if you feel the same way? In their simplicity and poetry both these sections are intensely moving. Then the wordless choruses interested us greatly. We have heard nothing like it before. I think you are the first to have tried such an experiment. I think a lot more of this kind of thing, quite original effects, might be done.

Hans Haym and Delius with the score of *A Mass of Life.*

To BARTÓK . . . *music should be . . . flowing purely from one's own feeling and without too much intellectuality.—So, feeling! I put forward Berlioz and Strauss as purely intellectual composers. In spite of their technical perfection and many other interesting points, both lack for me what is the soul of music—They try to make up for it by purely superficial means—I feel you are cut out for something quite different—*

Wordless chorus from *A Mass of Life.*

A Village Romeo and Juliet had reached London in 1910. Now, with another opera, *Fennimore and Gerda*, behind him, Delius turned in 1911 to a further orchestral work exploiting the wordless chorus which so interested Bartók. This was *The Song of the High Hills*. Another major work composed this year was *An Arabesk*, to a poem by Jacobsen.

Delius's friendship with another young admirer, Philip Heseltine (later known as Peter Warlock), also dates from 1911. Heseltine's many subsequent piano reductions of Delius's increasingly elaborate scores reveal his subtle and detailed craftsmanship.

Philip Heseltine.

From Heseltine's MS piano arrangement of *Lebenstanz*.

Two fine miniatures, the impressionistic *Summer Night on the River* and *On hearing the first Cuckoo in Spring*, date from 1911 and 1912. These, however, were years when a decline in his health first became clearly marked.

JELKA DELIUS to ADINE O'NEILL
Fred is now very much better—but still he needs constant care and looking after and I am by nature so anxious for him . . . The cure in Dresden only made Fred worse—awfully thin and haggard and he only picked up in Wiesbaden and everybody thinks he looks very well now. . . . He had quite overrated his nerves . . .

The only major work now to come before the outbreak of war is *North Country Sketches*; and a note of cool and spare astringency is introduced into his music.

**Characteristic of the period too is
a growing asperity in his
judgments.**

To GRANVILLE BANTOCK
*The Musical League I suppose is dead . . . I am afraid artistic undertakings
are impossible in England—The country is not yet artistically civilised—There
is something hopeless about English people in a musical and artistic way, to be
frank, I have entirely lost my interest and prefer to live abroad and make
flying visits—*

PHILIP HESELTINE on the first performance of *Songs of Sunset* at a Delius
Concert given by Beecham
I cannot adequately express in words what intense pleasure it was to
me to hear such perfect performances of such perfect music . . .
I cannot thank you enough for allowing me to meet you and for the most
glorious evening I have ever spent.

PHILIP HESELTINE
I spend most of my time saturating myself with Delius's music. I am
sure there is no music more beautiful in all the world; it haunts me day
and night—it is always with me and seems, by its continual presence, to
intensify the beauty of everything else for me.

To PHILIP HESELTINE *It is of no importance whether you write at the piano
or not as long as you feel you want to express some emotion. Music is nothing
else.*

**An encounter with Stravinsky demonstrates a continuing interest in the
works of younger composers.**

To IGOR STRAVINSKY
*I am afraid it is quite impossible for me to come to the dress rehearsal
tomorrow, but I shall certainly come on Thursday as I insist on hearing your
work: only as I haven't a ticket I shall call for you at your hotel to go in with
you as I did last time . . . Your music interests me enormously, something I
cannot say for most of the music I have heard for a very long time.*

IGOR STRAVINSKY
I met Frederick Delius. He had come to Covent Garden to attend a
performance of our Ballet. Beecham introduced him to me, and he paid me
compliments for *Petroushka*, but, as I spoke almost no English, and he but
little French, the conversation did not develop. Thirty-seven years later, I
visited his famous orange farm, D. H. Lawrence's would-have-been Utopia,
in Florida.

**In 1912 Delius had sold Solana Grove to Hans Haym, whose son Rudolf
was despatched to try his luck in Florida. Probably the last meeting with
his old friend came in March 1914, when the Deliuses went to Elberfeld
to hear the *Songs of Sunset* performed by the Elberfeld Choral Society, to
whom the work was dedicated.**

Igor Stravinsky.

**With Jelka and Ida Gerhardi at
the home of Consul
Max Esser, Elberfeld 1914.**

The War and after, 1914–23

The Deliuses travelled to England shortly after the outbreak of war and remained there for over a year. Composition continued, and one of the first new works to be completed was a Concerto for Violin and Cello, written for May and Beatrice Harrison.

Beatrice Harrison.

From the autograph MS of the Violin and Cello Concerto.

After their return to France, a feature of the war years was the deepening friendship with a wealthy American couple in Paris: the sculptor Henry Clews and his wife Marie. In 1916 Clews executed a fine mask of Delius.

JELKA DELIUS to MARIE CLEWS
I should love to see the mask of Fred. How splendid it will be!

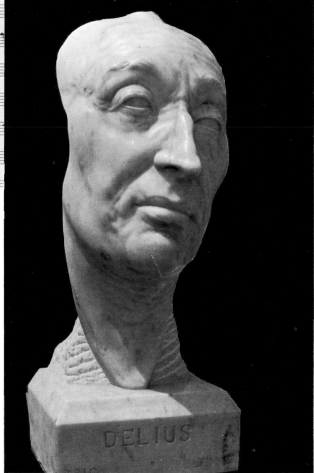

JELKA DELIUS to MARIE CLEWS
. . . we are happy indeed that you understand our life and are our friends, both of you.

The Deliuses with Henry Clews at Grez.

At the piano at Grez.

From a sketch for Part IV of the *Requiem* 'To the
memory of all young Artists fallen in the war'.

Inevitably the war brought problems. German royalties dried up—a major blow to a composer whose works had mainly been published in Germany—and performances dwindled. A growing belief that America might hold the future hope for his music was encouraged by Grainger, who had recently emigrated there and who set about promoting Delius with his customary zeal. A still greater worry than finance was his uncertain health; this did not, however, preclude an almost febrile creative activity during the war years.

PERCY GRAINGER, from New York
Quite apart from my efforts, I can see there's going to be a boom in Delius here anyhow. People ask me about you and talk about you fifty times more than they did 6 months ago.

LEOPOLD STOKOWSKI
. . . for the last week I have been studying his 'Messe des Lebens'. This is a work planned on an enormously large scale and interests me very deeply . . . such a monumental work as this would need a great deal of preparation . . . Percy Grainger and I have often discussed Delius, and I am hoping soon to hear him play his piano concerto.

JELKA DELIUS to MARIE CLEWS
I have been very troubled about him. He was really not at all well lately . . . He always forbids me to say that anything is the matter with him . . . He felt so very weak and low and depressed—

Maud Cunard wrote me yesterday—Beecham is in great financial difficulties—the estate of his father cannot be wound up for 2 or 3 years and he seems to be without money entirely and of course he cannot fulfil his contract with me—We are taking the Gauguin to London in order to try and sell it—If we dont succeed I shall have to try and make a loan.

JELKA DELIUS to MARIE CLEWS, Biarritz, July 1918.
Fred has been working splendidly and has quite finished his Symphony. He calls it 'A poem of Life and Love', and it is really that, so emotional and warm and flowering forth so wonderfully! He has also done another short piece for small orchestra, a Song before Sunrise which is quite charming too—Oh, how I wish you could see him so well, his eyes so *entirely* alright again. It is the greatest blessing.

During the war I wrote a great deal, almost incessantly; I completed my 'Pagan Requiem'. A Concerto for Violin, Violoncello and Orchestra. A Violin Concerto—A Cello Sonata—A ballad for Orchestra Eventyr (once upon a time) after Asbjørnsens folklore—A Dance Rhapsody (No 2)—A string quartet—A Poem of Life and Love for Orchestra—A Song before Sunrise for small Orchestra—4 Elizabethan songs—2 a capella partsongs—

The summer of 1918, spent at Biarritz in the rue Gardague, was a fruitful period.

The outbreak of war had halted plans to produce *Fennimore and Gerda* in Germany. It was finally staged in Frankfurt in October 1919. Based on J. P. Jacobsen's novel *Niels Lyhne* the work may be seen almost as a musical counterpart to Edvard Munch's painting, an impression starkly strengthened by the cover design to the vocal score, published the same year. Munch's own striking portrait of the composer was executed a little later.

FERRUCCIO BUSONI to his wife

Delius has come back from Frankfurt, full of enthusiasm. He is the first to bring good news from Germany. His 'Niels Lyhne' was performed there at great expense and with much care . . . It was a relief to hear something good about Germany for once . . .

JELKA DELIUS to MARIE CLEWS

In Frankfort we stayed a month and assisted all the rehearsals and first performance of 'Fennimore and Gerda'. It was a great thing after all those years of waiting. We are very happy because the thing is beautiful and all Fred intended comes off perfectly—

. . . length and cumbrousness, in my opinion, will be the first features to disappear, and that is the end towards which I am working—brevity and conciseness. Long dialogue and wearisome narrations must go, and will be replaced by short, strong emotional impressions given in a series of terse scenes. Ninety minutes to two hours is long enough for any opera, and by reducing intervals, as I have done in my own work, to three minutes instead of the usual half-hour necessitated by ponderous realistic decoration, this limit can easily be preserved.

Early sketch for *Fennimore and Gerda.*

The Composer Delius, by Edvard Munch.

THOMAS BEECHAM

A final word on the non-lyrical nature of the whole piece. The composer said to me at the time that in his opinion he had eliminated from it all that was unessential to the true development both of the drama and the music. Let us hope that this sweeping elimination may not have been carried a step too far.

Jealousy, by Edvard Munch.

The Composer Delius at Wiesbaden, by Edvard Munch.

The early twenties were quieter years, with Delius's health being only precariously maintained. The last meetings with Munch in 1920 and 1922 brought intense pleasure. Norway itself was explored afresh and in 1921 Delius had a cottage, 'Høifagerli,' built there, at Lesjaskog in Gudbrandsdalen.

JELKA DELIUS to PHILIP HESELTINE
He has not been so very well lately and this constant anxiety about the money makes him so nervous . . .

EDVARD MUNCH
I am so glad that I have seen you and your wife again . . . I saw a lot of old friends again in Paris this year—I went and visited old places.—I thought of the poor but beautiful time when I had my studio in the rue de la Santé—I remembered the time when I tried to sell old wine bottles in order to get something to eat—And I could not even get 10 centimes for them. You remember how in those days I often had a midday meal with you—drank good wine and you revived me with your good humour—At that time you also took me to Molard where they were so kind to me—All my acquaintances have become very old—Molard was quite venerable—

. . . you have kept that optimistic good humour for which I have often envied you—He who has this strong inner self is happier than so many others—

JELKA DELIUS to MARIE CLEWS
Lady C[unard] had a young Italian sculptor (Secessionist from Rome called Riccardi) and she got him to make a bust of Fred. It was really awfully fine and full of character . . .

JAPPE NILSSEN to EDVARD MUNCH at Wiesbaden.
If you meet Delius and his wife, do give them my regards; it was sad to hear that things aren't well with him.

In the garden at Grez with his
sister Clare.

and with Jelka.

Ida and William Molard outside
their studio in Paris.

**The round of cures had now begun. Walking was
becoming difficult and Delius had increasingly to
use a wheelchair.**

JELKA DELIUS to ADINE O'NEILL, Lesjaskog,
Gudbrandsdalen, July 1922
It is rather a physical breakdown, mentally he is as
fresh and vivacious as ever, but his legs and arms are
so very weak and might, if we had not begun a cure
immediately, have been paralysed altogether.
. . . his weakness came on gradually in the course of a
month, after he had for some years been more or less
weak in his limbs . . .

We are quite delighted with our little hut up here—it
was a tremendous moment, when we saw it standing
quite finished on the hillside, after we had only
designed the plan before leaving last year.

JELKA DELIUS to PERCY GRAINGER
I am sending you a little collection of photos from
Høifagerli, which, I hope, you will like.

Delius, by Max Beckmann.

at Dr Simon, Untermainkai 5,
Jan 29, 1923

Frederick Delius
(geb. 29. Januar 1863)

I.

Nordlandskizzen (1913-14)
 Vier Orchesterstücke
  (Für Klavier zu vier Händen bearbeitet von Ph. Heseltine)
  1) Der Herbstwind säuselt in den Bäumen. 2) Winter-
  landschaft. 3) Tanz. 4) Frühlingseinzug.

Eventyr (1917)
 Ballade für Orchester nach altnordischen Volkssagen.
  (Für Klavier zu vier Händen bearbeitet v. B. J. Dale)
 Herr Alexander Lippay, Herr Paul Meyer.

II.

Lieder für Sopran
 Das Veilchen (Ludwig Holstein)
 Seidenschuhe (J. P. Jacobsen)
 Schwarze Rosen (Josephson)
 Nachtigall (Henley)
 Frühlingslied (J. P. Jacobsen)

 Frau Sibby Freund
 Am Klavier: Herr Paul Meyer

III.

Tanz-Rhapsodie (für Orchester. 1908)
 (Für zwei Klaviere bearbeitet von Percy Grainger)
 Herr Percy Grainger, Herr Alexander Lippay.

There is really only one quality for great music and that is 'emotion'—Look with what ease hundreds of young composers are quietly expressing themselves in the so-called 'new idiom'. Otherwise the wrong note system—Hundreds of painters are seeing in Cubes—But it all means nothing more than a fashion—and surely intellectual when at its best.

I, myself, am entirely at a loss to explain how I compose—I know only that at first I conceive a work suddenly—thro' a feeling—the work appears to me instantaneously as a whole, but as a feeling—the working out of the whole work in detail is then easy as long as I have the feeling—the emotion—it becomes difficult as the emotion becomes less keen; sometimes I am obliged to put the work aside for months—sometimes years—and take it up again, having almost, or entirely, forgotten it; in order to bring back my first feeling.

Music is a cry of the soul. It is a revelation, a thing to be reverenced. Performances of a great musical work are for us what the rites and festivals of religion were to the ancients—an initiation into the mysteries of the human soul.

It was for Heseltine soon to make the curious discovery that Delius was actually born a year earlier than everyone—including Delius himself—had thought. Not, however, in time for his sixtieth birthday, celebrated at the age of 61 in Frankfurt at the home of a close friend, Dr Heinrich Simon, proprietor of the *Frankfurter Zeitung*.

JELKA DELIUS to the CLEWS

. . . we are here in quite a media[e]val house just under the Cathedral for the winter months as there are quite a number of Delius performances coming on. Especially a Delius-concert on March 1st and Elroy Flecker's Drama 'Hassan' at Darmstadt with Delius' musique de scène.
On the 29th of this month he will be sixty and we are surrounded here by delightful and friendly musicians, poets and also Beckmann, a great German painter: They are giving a chamber-music concert on that day as a surprise at the house of a great friend. Percy Grainger is here and will play some of his things. New songs will be sung, Binding the Poet has translated a Verlaine song most admirably, all this will be heartwarming for him.

JELKA DELIUS to ADINE O'NEILL

I am sorry the winter here is ended, we had such a delightful time. Percy Grainger is with us a lot and a delightful friend. Also several other young musicians and composers from here were awfully nice and spent many evenings here—and on the 1st of March they gave a Delius Concert.

Percy Grainger's copy of the Birthday Recital programme.

At the piano at Grez.

With Jelka and Percy Grainger in Frankfurt, 5 April 1923.

With Lloyd Osbourne at Grez.

Financial worries were greatly eased by the extraordinarily successful London run, beginning in September 1923, of James Elroy Flecker's *Hassan*, for which Delius had been specially commissioned to write incidental music.

Increasing weakness and failing eyesight now meant that Delius had more and more to rely on the help of others. Jelka and Philip Heseltine helped to write down his music, and Jelka was now accustomed to taking down his letters by dictation. In the summer, on the last visit to Norway, Grainger came and himself contributed a short dance movement required for the purposes of the London production of *Hassan*.

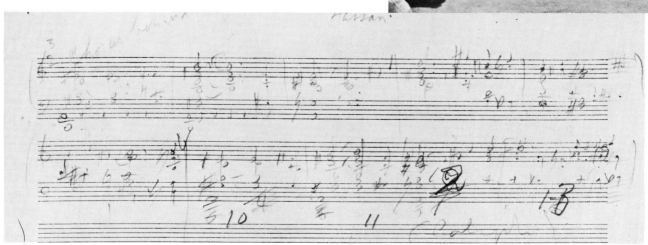

Sketch for chorus from *Hassan*, one of the last MSS from Delius's own hand.

The same passage in the hand of Philip Heseltine from the full score.

His Majesty's Theatre.

Centre: **Scene from the London production of** *Hassan.*

JELKA DELIUS to MARIE CLEWS
It has been a great success—the place is always booked for weeks and months ahead; and this great publicity of course has done Delius's fame a lot of good. I am glad we went to London.

To PERCY GRAINGER *We were 9 days in London and attended 2 rehearsals and 2 performances. The whole show is really magnificent, wonderful scenery, lighting and costumes and I understand now that there was too little music before I had written the additions, especially for the last 2 scenes, where music goes on almost all the time. The leaving of the Caravan, the gradual disappearing made a wonderful effect and was beautifully realized by the chorusses on and behind the scene. In fact all chorusses were excellent. Our ballet piece was a* great success *and brought just a vigorous contrast to the rest. The serenade sounded* very well *pizzicato and a muted violin playing the melody. It is then sung later on with the tenor voice and orchestra. I have discarded the Piano altogether. Afterwards it comes once more as an entr'acte for full orchestra—also very good. But of course a real artistic atmosphere is unobtainable as the public chats, drinks tea, eats chocolates as soon as the curtain drops and the actors insist on coming out after every scene, instead of only after the big acts. The piece, tho', seems to have been a very great success and the advance-booking has beaten all records of London theatres.*

JELKA DELIUS to PERCY GRAINGER
When we were in London Elliot and Fry's made some quite good photo's of Delius. Would you like them for publicity? The negatives are at Elliot and Fry's but I could get copies made?

The measure of Grainger's devotion and support during these early years of infirmity remained undiminished.

Grainger and Delius.

Jelka, Percy Grainger and Delius.

To PERCY GRAINGER *We were wondering, whether ever any other composer had met with a colleague and friend like you, so devoted and interested in his friend's work and understanding it thro' his own genius.*

The financial success of *Hassan* meant that Jelka could take her husband to the winter sunshine of Mediterranean shores in her anxious search for a cure for his illness.

JELKA DELIUS to PERCY GRAINGER
It is beastly cold here now and we are busy packing up to go to Rapallo near Genoa for the winter. We have taken Gordon Craig's little house . . .

Rapallo.

The last decade, 1924–34

The winter at Rapallo was spent quietly, enlivened by visits from Balfour Gardiner and Arnold Bax and by the presence of Max Beerbohm, a near neighbour. Delius's health improved and there was an idyllic month in the spring at La Napoule, near Cannes, where Henry and Marie Clews were restoring the Château that they had recently purchased.

JELKA DELIUS to MARIE CLEWS, Rapallo, March 1924. Fred loves the idea of staying there [in La Napoule], as he is in the middle of composing an orchestral work and feels that in such genial surroundings and with you, dear friends so near, he could almost finish it.

With Marie Clews at the Château de La Napoule.

With Jelka at the Château de La Napoule.

The Château de La Napoule during renovation in the 1920s.

JELKA DELIUS to the CLEWS
We enjoyed being near you so immensely and our true home was not 'Les Brisants' but your beloved garden smiling to us in all its moods; and you dear people made our stay so delightful.

A feature of the next two years was the painful and dispiriting trek from the one spa or *Kurort* to the next. But by the mid-twenties Delius was completely blind and paralysed. With one notable exception there were to be no more major excursions from Grez; and the visits of friends who made music now became high points of the year.

JELKA DELIUS to MARIE CLEWS

I have thought of you often, but I thought that all the world knew of Fred's sad state: *he can not see at all.* We have passed a terrible winter in Cassel, trying to save his eyes and seeing them get worse and worse, trying all specialists etc, at last we came back here end of May and since then his general state is *slightly* improved, but not the eyes. He therefore cannot walk at all. We have a man who carries him up and down, and he lies most of the day in the garden on his chaiselongue. That lovely garden all full of flowers and he cannot see it! His mind is lucid and as active as ever and of course to keep him from depression I read to him a tremendous lot. But best of all, a few weeks ago Balfour Gardiner and Percy Grainger came together and played to him on 2 pianos and also the great Cellist Barjansky came to Grez to spend the holidays and we had wonderful concerts every day. It seemed to do Fred wonderfully much good . . .

CATHERINE BARJANSKY

Delius was a ghost, emaciated, bloodless, his long body as stiff as a corpse. There was great spiritual beauty in his face, the forehead high and noble, the eyes unusually deep-set, the eyelids heavy and half closed, the nose thin and aquiline, the mouth fine and beautiful in shape. His narrow pale hands lay helpless on his knees. His gray hair was long, so long that it fell over the open collar of his white silk sport shirt, revealing his long thin neck with a large Adam's apple. He did not wear a necktie; his suit was of light Shantung; his shoes were white suède. Everything about his appearance betrayed the great and thoughtful care his wife had given it. And despite his helplessness, he looked extremely elegant. I realized that he was almost completely paralyzed.

CATHERINE BARJANSKY

I had some wax with me and I began to model his expressive face, though I asked Mrs Delius not to let him know it. Because he was so completely motionless it was easy to model him, and during the two hours we spent in his room, while his attention was wholly absorbed by his conversation with my husband, I could move around him without his noticing it and model him from every side.

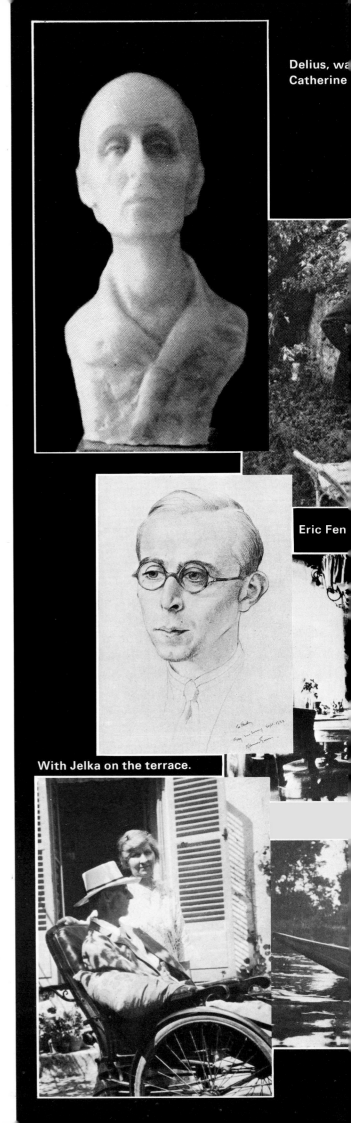

Delius, wa
Catherine

Eric Fen

With Jelka on the terrace.

e by
.

n the garden at Grez: Percy
Grainger with his fiancée Ella
Viola Ström and Balfour Gardiner.

es Gunn.

Interior of the house at Grez.

A boating party on the Loing:
Jelka, Catherine and Alexandre
Barjansky, and Percy Grainger.

1928: the flood of composition is a memory. Delius had written virtually nothing for five years and several works, some little more than sketches, lay unfinished and gathering the dust in the stillness of a silent house.

JELKA DELIUS to MARIE CLEWS
We are . . . living our calm and almost posthumous existence, and longing for spring!

In August there came a letter from a young music student in Yorkshire which was to make an unexpected impact on the last six years of his life.

ERIC FENBY
. . . the conceit that I could help became an obsession . . . and in the end I could not sleep for it. Finally it conquered me, and, getting up in the middle of the night, I took pen and paper and wrote to Delius offering my help for three or four years. I would do anything to be the means of his finishing that music . . .

I am greatly touched by your kind and sympathetic letter and should love to accept your offer. Come here by all means as soon as you can and see if you like it before deciding anything . . . We live very simply here—No grand clothes needed.

The spring of 1929 brought a signal honour from his native country, where news of fresh attempts at composition with the help of Fenby helped to create a revival of interest in his music. Performances of his works on the radio, with Adrian Boult and others applying pressure to have Delius's compositions broadcast on BBC wavelengths best received in France, were a marvellous bonus.

JELKA DELIUS to MARIE CLEWS
. . . Fred has been made a 'Companion of Honour'; it is supposed to be a great distinction, as there are only 30 or 40 living C.H.'s. It was founded after the war. Fred would have refused a knighthood . . .
There were also fearful faked interviews in the Press, saying this made Fred the happiest man in the world.—Of course quite untrue—and just about the last thing Fred would say or think.—
No, he has kept his aloof dignity—in fact he has now a calm beauty and serenity that are quite wonderful. When the people of the world sit near him gushing they look quite horrid caricatures and so much older, pleated and yellow than he does that I am amazed at their courage, talking nonsense to him.

JELKA DELIUS to MARIE CLEWS
As to the Radio . . . we have heard hundreds of performances of Delius on it, and some really marvellously good . . . I leave you to imagine how dear Fred storms when I cannot find a station, or get a bad audition and crackings, and how desperately I sit before all this electrical machinery when something is wrong. Imagine me absolutely terrified. And altho' I have no technical gifts at all, I have become really very efficient out of the ardent wish to give Fred pleasure . . . P.S. My hair is perfectly white now—it does not look too bad.

Beecham, Heseltine and other friends were now laying the groundwork in London for an event that would be unique by any standards: a Festival of six concerts devoted entirely to his works. Hoping that Delius's health would withstand the strain Jelka made arrangements in October for a long and painful journey.

QUEEN'S HALL

Sole Lessees - Messrs. CHAPPELL & Co., Ltd.

Delius Festival

Conductor and Organiser :

Sir THOMAS BEECHAM

First Concert

(Given under the auspices of the Columbia Graphophone Co., Ltd.)

SATURDAY, OCTOBER 12th, 1929

at 3 p.m.

PAULINE MAUNDER

HEDDLE NASH

DENNIS NOBLE

THE LONDON SELECT CHOIR

(Conductor - T. ARNOLD FULTON)

and a specially selected orchestra conducted by

Sir THOMAS BEECHAM

Principal Violin :

CHARLES WOODHOUSE

1

DELIUS FESTIVAL

Conductor and Organiser - SIR THOMAS BEECHAM, Bart.

REMAINING CONCERTS

(1) ÆOLIAN HALL Wednesday Evening, October 16th at 8.30

Sir Thomas Beecham will conduct a specially selected Orchestra of 30 performers.
THE FIRST CUCKOO—SUMMER NIGHT—AIR AND DANCE (first performance)—SONG BEFORE SUNRISE—CELLO SONATA—SONGS AND PIANO PIECES
The soloists will include Miss Beatrice Harrison ('Cello), Mr. Evlyn Howard-Jones (Pianoforte), Miss Olga Haley (Mezzo-Soprano), Mr. John Armstrong (Tenor) and Mr. John Goss (Baritone).

(2) QUEEN'S HALL Friday Evening, October 18th at 8
(Sole Lessees—Messrs. Chappell & Co. Ltd.)

Choral and Orchestral Concert, given by the British Broadcasting Corporation
EVENTYR—ARABESK (first performance)—PIANO CONCERTO—CYNARA (first performance)—APPALACHIA
Sir Thomas Beecham will conduct the London Select Choir and the British Broadcasting Orchestra. The soloists will be Mr. John Goss (Baritone) and Mr. Evlyn Howard-Jones (Pianoforte).

(3) ÆOLIAN HALL Wednesday Evening, October 23rd at 8.30
STRING QUARTET—VIOLIN SONATA (No. 1)—SONGS and PART-SONGS
The London Select Choir, The Virtuoso String Quartet, Mr. Arthur Catterall (Violin) Mr. Evlyn Howard-Jones (Pianoforte), Miss Dora Labbette (Soprano) and Mr. Heddle Nash (Tenor).

(4) QUEEN'S HALL Thursday Evening, October 24th at 8
(Sole Lessees— Messrs. Chappell & Co. Ltd.)

Choral and Orchestral Concert, given by the Royal Philharmonic Society
NORTH-COUNTRY SKETCHES—SONGS OF SUNSET—VIOLIN CONCERTO—DANCE RHAPSODY (No. 1)—GERDA (first performance in England)
Sir Thomas Beecham will conduct the London Select Choir and the Royal Philharmonic Orchestra. The soloists will include Miss Olga Haley (Mezzo-Soprano), Miss Pauline Maunder (Soprano), Mr. Leyland White (Baritone) and Mr. Albert Sammons (Violin).

(5) QUEEN'S HALL Friday Evening, November 1st at 8
(Sole Lessees— Messrs. Chappell & Co. Ltd.)

Choral and Orchestral Concert, given by the British Broadcasting Corporation
"A MASS OF LIFE"
Sir Thomas Beecham will conduct the Philharmonic Choir and the British Broadcasting Orchestra. The soloists will include Miss Miriam Licette (Soprano), Miss Astra Desmond (Contralto), Mr. Tudor Davies (Tenor) and Mr. Roy Henderson (Baritone).

Reserved Seats: **12/-, 9/6, 5/9.** Unreserved: **3/6 and 2/4.** Prices include tax.

Tickets for any or all of the Concerts may be obtained from Messrs. Chappell's Box Office, Queen's Hall, Langham Place, W.1 or from the Box Office, Aeolian Hall, New Bond Street, W.1.

32

2 pages from the programme of the first Festival Concert.

The Queen's Hall, from Langham Place.

THE TRIBUTE TO DELIUS.

BLIND COMPOSER'S RAPTURE.

By ROBIN H. LEGGE.

Many of the vast multitude which packed Queen's Hall on Saturday afternoon, when the Delius Festival began, must have been at least surprised when, at the end, the composer bowed his head over and over again and gently waved his arms in acknowledgment of the storms of applause which greeted him; the old bright and rather amused smile lay upon his handsome countenance, that I at least have been privileged to know for close upon half a century. For have not the tales that were told of the great composer's utter helplessness been so harrowing and in fact so misleading as to induce the belief that Frederick Delius would be seen, like Elizabeth in "Tannhäuser," at full length upon a bier?

How different the reality! The composer, who had arrived in Queen's Hall in a chair, was found, when the public were admitted, to be seated in an armchair in the Grand Circle, from which a few seats had been barred off in order to give him, his wife, and his attendant sufficient space in which to be comfortable. So alert is his mind that when

Frederick Delius at the Queen's Hall, by Ernest Procter.

The first concert included *Brigg Fair, Dance Rhapsody No. 2, Sea Drift, In a Summer Garden,* excerpts from *A Village Romeo and Juliet,* and the first performance of a work completed with Fenby's help, *A Late Lark.*

At the Festival with Philip Heseltine *(left)* and Jelka.

DELIUS, speaking at the close of the final concert
Thank you for the very fine reception you have given me . . . This Festival has been the time of my life . . .

JELKA DELIUS to ERIC FENBY Grez, December 1929.
He is quite well, his appetite is better than before, and I think upon the whole the trip has done him good.

JELKA DELIUS to PERCY GRAINGER
He has been more lively and active mentally since the great stir of the Festival . . .

The peak of the collaboration with Fenby was reached in 1930, with the completion of *A Song of Summer* and the writing of a violin sonata and a large-scale work for chorus and orchestra, *Songs of Farewell*, the latter premièred in London in 1932.

With Eric Fenby at Grez, after the completion of *Songs of Farewell*.

JELKA DELIUS to ERNEST NEWMAN
After the 3rd Violin Sonata Fred tackled a work for Double Chorus and Orchestra with words by Walt Whitman. They are five short poems or fragments, from the late poems of W.W. and all allude to the Sea and to the Departure on the ultimate voyage. He calls it 'The last voyage'. This work was entirely sketched out in 1921 or 20, when he put it aside to do the Hassan Music. Now that Eric Fenby had got to be so wonderfully adept at working for him he was able to finish it. It was marvellous how he would have it all in his head and think of slight changes in the orchestration over night, or of quite new bits, when he would sometimes dictate over twenty bars in one swing. Fenby helped him splendidly, and I don't know anyone who could have been so perfect.

From the MS of the full score of *Songs of Farewell*, in Eric Fenby's hand.

Jelka's hope that Edvard Munch would come to Grez to paint his old friend gradually faded as the ageing artist spun his own web of loneliness in the fastness of his home in Norway. But among a number of English artists of distinction who depicted Delius in the last five years of his life were Augustus John and James Gunn.

JELKA DELIUS to ERIC FENBY
I am sending you a beautiful photo of Delius, which the little Photographer in Fontainebleau did. It is marvellous; I worked him up to such a pitch that he quite surpassed himself and was overcome with surprise at his achievement. He did it here in the room too and it was a miracle that a very bright cloud came right opposite the glass door at the moment.

JELKA DELIUS to EDVARD MUNCH
When I look at him I always have to think of *you*, for I always feel that *no-one* could make a picture of him as *you* could. He is now so handsome, so expressive, calm, original. You could paint or draw that so splendidly. Please, please, when you are again in these parts, do come and paint him. Here you have peace, a studio, and good red wine and us two, your loyal friends . . . *you must paint* the picture of the sick Delius. You will make a masterpiece of it.

EDVARD MUNCH
I have thought about making a short trip to Paris—but not until summer. But it is uncertain—It was to visit you and other friends—I would have painted you then. It would have been a very beautiful picture.

JELKA DELIUS to PERCY GRAINGER
We are now all the time thinking of the 1st performance of his 'Songs of Farewell' at the Courtauld Sargent Concerts on the 21st and 22d. This work is by far *the crown* of all he has achieved with Fenby. If only the dashy and tempestuous Malcolm Sargent can conduct it right! But happily Fenby is up in London; this work is the apple of his eye and he will do all he can to help Sargent.

Frederick Delius, by Augustus John.

Elgar Visits Delius

BLIND COMPOSER BUSY ON NEW WORK

From Our Own Correspondent

PARIS, Tuesday.

TWO giants of British music met at the home of one of them near Paris to-day, when Sir Edward Elgar, who has come to Paris to conduct the performance of his violin concerto, motored out on a pilgrimage to see the blind and paralysed composer, Delius.

The two great musicians warmly greeted each other, and remained for over two hours in animated conversation. The contrast between the erect and vigorous figure of Sir Edward and the thin and emaciated figure of Delius was a pathetic one.

MENTAL VIGOUR

"I was delighted to find my old friend in far better health than I had been led to expect," said Sir Edward. "Delius during the whole of my visit was bright and mentally vigorous and keenly interested in everything going on in the musical world. He is actually composing at the present time."

Delius explained at length to Sir Edward the scheme of a new work for baritone, chorus and orchestra on which he is now engaged.

Sir Edward Elgar brought with him a collection of records of contemporary British singers, so that Delius might choose the type best suited to his new music.

Finally Sir Edward brought a new ray of hope into the blind composer's life.

"Now you can fly to London in a couple of hours," he said.

"That means I can go there very often," replied Delius, and his face lighted up.

The last time Delius crossed to England to attend a performance of his work the journey took him three days by boat and by ambulance.

Sir Edward Elgar is returning to London by air on Thursday morning.

PHILIP OYLER

He would sit down and start to draw. In a few minutes Delius would change his position. Gunn would start again, and this would go on throughout the time allotted for the sitting. Exasperating, of course for Gunn, but Delius could not sit in any one position for more than a short time, as it became too painful for him and he had to move.

I suggested tentatively, that during a sitting Gunn might study and memorise the natural pose of head or hand and convey it to canvas afterwards at leisure, and this indeed is what he was compelled to do, and if this portrait falls short of other work done by him there is every possible excuse why it should. As Delius always had a rug draped over his legs, this did not present the same difficulty. Eric Fenby's legs, covered by the usual rug, served this purpose and he could sit as desired.

In 1932, another honour came from England, the Freedom of his native Bradford. The major composition of the year was the *Idyll*, using some of the material from the long-discarded *Margot la Rouge*.

JELKA DELIUS to the CLEWS

I have now got such a technique in describing things to him that he with his wonderful imagination sees it all. Sunsets and rising moons on the river and the funny people of Grez.

Not being able to see does not trouble me. I have my imagination. Besides I have seen the best of the earth and done everything that is worth doing; I am content. I have had a wonderful life.

The most poignant meeting of all was with Elgar, himself a sick man, who had come with Menuhin to Paris at the end of May 1933 for a performance of his Violin Concerto. He made the pilgrimage to Grez, from which there sprang a late-flowering friendship all too quickly cut short by his death the following February.

EDWARD ELGAR

I am supposed to be improving and want to share a few more years with you and hear your 'brave transluminary things' and to see and talk once more with the poet's mind in the poet's body—you in fact.

To ERNEST NEWMAN

His visit to me here when he spent an afternoon with me was quite an event in my life. It was the first time that the real Elgar was revealed to me and that I could talk intimately with him and that I had the opportunity of appreciating his fine intellect and affectionate nature. How I now regret that we were not brought together earlier!

EDWARD ELGAR

I still have a vivid memory of Mrs. Delius and you and I hold it one of the few happy events in my life.

To THOMAS BEECHAM, 17 December 1933

When am I to have the records of Appalachia, Paris, the Idyll and Songs of Farewell etc.? I am just longing to be able to put them on my gramophone. This is now my only pleasure. Don't wait too long, dear friend, or it will be too late for me to enjoy them.

Bouts of pain, relieved by morphine, increased in intensity as the cruel decline of 1934 set in. The death of another friend, Norman O'Neill, in March, was a bitter blow. In May, Jelka sent a telegram to Fenby, now back in England, to call him to Delius's bedside while she herself underwent an operation for cancer. The end came on 10 June 1934. Within the space of a few months English music had lost its giants, Elgar, Holst and Delius.

DELIUS, THE COMPOSER, DEAD

Tragedy of a Neglected Genius

FIGHT TO FAME—AND THEN BLINDNESS

The "Daily Mirror" regrets to announce the death of Frederick Delius, one of Britain's greatest composers, at his home at Grez-sur-Loing, near Paris, yesterday.

DELIUS, who was seventy-two, and had been blind for the past six years, died after a long illness, during which he suffered greatly. "Death came as a relief," said a close friend, according to a Reuter message from Paris last night.

Mrs. Delius, who was herself an invalid, following an operation ten days ago, had been hastily recalled from the nursing home to her dying husband's side and was with him at the last.

It is understood that the body will later be taken to England.

After the death had been announced in the B.B.C. news bulletin last night an orchestra played the "Walk to the Paradise Garden" from the composer's "A Village Romeo and Juliet."

Delius is the third British composer to die in the last four months, for Elgar passed away in February and Gustav Holst in May. Elgar, his contemporary and friend, visited him only a year ago at Grez, where he had lived for the past thirty years in almost complete retirement.

In Honours List

Though famous in Germany, Delius until a few years ago was almost unknown in England, despite the fact that he was a native of Bradford, and had it not been for Sir Thomas Beecham his works would have remained practically unplayed in this country.

Britain was reminded in 1929 that a genius was being allowed to languish in obscurity, paralysed and on the verge of total blindness, by the appearance of his name in the Honours List as a Companion of Honour.

A festival of his works was given the same year at Queen's Hall under the direction of Sir Thomas Beecham, who described him as the greatest British musician since Purcell, and he attended the six concerts in an ambulance.

It is Delius who has given the world a profound a picture in music of English air and sky, cliffs, green lawns and golden light, as did Spenser, Chaucer, or Wordsworth in verse.

Some of his most popular works are "A Mass of Life," the opera "A Village Romeo and Juliet," "Appalachia," "Sea Drift," "Songs of Sunset," "Paris," "Brigg Fair," "Life's Dance" and the incidental music to "Hassan."

Mind-reading Music

For years he had been working with the aid of an amanuensis, Eric Fenby.

By something like thought reading Mr. Fenby recorded on paper what was in the mind of Delius, whose voice could not express more than a feeble monotone and whose hands were useless.

A story of unusual interest attaches to the age of Delius.

Until November, 1929, he had gone through life in the belief that he was a year younger than he was, and reference books gave the date of his birth as 1863.

It was Peter Warlock, his friend and biographer, who discovered he was born on January 29, 1862. No one was more surprised than Delius when Warlock told him, and for more than two years the secret remained with the composer and his wife.

An accomplished violinist when he was ten, Delius admitted he was a self-taught musician, and said he owed a great debt to the negro music he heard when he was working at an orange-grove in Florida in the 'eighties.

Mr. Frederick Delius, the famous English composer, photographed with his wife.

Jelka died in London on 28 May 1935. Gravely ill she had brought Delius's body to London for reinterment at Limpsfield in Surrey. A few days later she was buried at his side.

The most precious part of this man is the immortal part—his spirit as revealed in his work; and in whatever sphere that spirit is, I should like our greetings to pass beyond the confines of this earthly sphere, and let him know that we are here, not in a spirit of vain regret, but rather in a spirit of rejoicing that his work is with us and will remain with us for evermore.

— From the funeral oration by Sir Thomas Beecham

Postscript

As far as possible this life has been related by the composer and his friends. The fact that much of the essence of Delius's life can be expressed in paintings, lithographs, and drawings is a measure of the man's involvement in the arts and artists in general, as opposed to music in particular. From the age of 26 his chosen homes, Paris and its suburbs, Ville d'Avray and Croissy, then Grez-sur-Loing, were or had been the haunts of artists too numerous to catalogue. So it occurred quite naturally that Edvard Munch, Ida Gerhardi, and Jelka Rosen came to play major roles in this book, and that Paul Gauguin, Alphonse Mucha, Auguste Rodin, Max Beckmann, John Singer Sargent, Augustus John, and others all figure in its pages.

This Life took shape gradually, as photographs and letters were sought out and chosen over a period of some years. But it was never intended to be a purely visual documentation, a pasting-up of externals. For this reason I invited Robert Threlfall to join me, aware that the book's musical dimension would be deepened and a better balance achieved. In the event the work has been rethought and has become very much a joint endeavour, to which designer Roger Davies has significantly contributed.

LIONEL CARLEY, London, January 1977.

Special acknowledgement is gratefully made to Chief Curator Arne Eggum, Curator Gerd Woll, and the trustees of the Munch Museum, Oslo; Professor George Loughlin, Archivist Kay Dreyfus, and the trustees of the Grainger Museum, Melbourne University; Frau Malve Steinweg and Fräulein Evelin Gerhardi, nieces of Ida Gerhardi; Eric Fenby; Mr and Mrs David J Colton of the Henry Clews La Napoule Art Foundation; Uta von Delius, Archivist to the Delius Family Association, Bielefeld; Frau Marie-Luise Baum; Bradford Art Galleries and Museums; Jeff Driggers of the Haydon Burns Library, Jacksonville; the staff of the Jacksonville University Library; members of the Delius Society, London and the Delius Association of Florida, Jacksonville; Jean-Michel Nectoux of the Bibliothèque Nationale, Paris; Wayne Shirley of the Library of Congress, Washington; the staff of the Royal Library, Stockholm, and the British Library, London; Rudolf Haym and the late Eva Haym-Simons; Madame A Merle d'Aubigné, Grez-sur-Loing; Stewart Manville and Ella Grainger; the late C W Orr; Pierre Bance; Lewis Foreman; Joan Pallister; Hans Peter Dieterling; Astrid Jägfeldt; David Rayner who supplied many of the postcard photographs; and Brian Lincoln, for preliminary photographic work.

For permission to reproduce Delius's published music our thanks go to Boosey and Hawkes Music Publishers Ltd; Oxford University Press Music Department; Stainer and Bell Ltd; and Universal Edition (London) Ltd.

A final expression of gratitude, to the members, past and present, of the Delius Trust, London: to the late Trustee, Dr Philip Emanuel, to whose memory this work is dedicated; his successor Major Norman Millar; Mr D Nott and Mr J A S Prouse of Barclays Bank Trust Company; Sir Thomas Armstrong; Felix Aprahamian; and Rachel Lowe Dugmore, who laid scholarly groundwork in her years as Archivist to the Trust. To them all we are indebted for their continuing interest and encouragement.

Further sources are acknowledged in the Notes, and items are reproduced by kind permission of the copyright owners wherever it has been possible to establish them. Four books are referred to more often than most: Sir Thomas Beecham: *Frederick Delius*, Hutchinson, London 1959; Clare Delius: *Frederick Delius, Memories of my Brother*, Ivor Nicholson and Watson, London 1935; Eric Fenby: *Delius as I Knew Him*, G Bell and Sons, London 1936; and Philip Heseltine: *Frederick Delius*, John Lane The Bodley Head, London 1923. In the Notes these are simply indicated by the author's name.

All translations from books, letters or documents originally in languages other than English are by Lionel Carley. Occasional idiosyncracies in spelling by Delius and his wife have generally been retained, and Delius's own writings are printed in italics throughout.

Sources of illustrations

i The Sun (detail), by Edvard Munch.
ii–iii: Frederick Delius in middle age. Photograph *Coll.* L. Carley.

1 Bradford in 1860, sketched from Cemetery Terrace. Print in the collection of the Local Studies Department, City Library, Bradford.

Nos 4–6 Claremont, Bradford, birthplace of Delius. Photograph by L. Carley, 1975.

2 Julius Friedrich Wilhelm Delius (1822–1901). Photograph by E. Passingham, Bradford. *Coll.* Familienverbindung Delius, Bielefeld.

Elise Pauline Delius, *née* Krönig (1838–1929). Photograph by E. Passingham, Bradford. *Coll.* Familienverbindung Delius, Bielefeld.

The Delius family house at No. 1 Claremont, Bradford. Photograph in programme for the Fourth Concert of the Delius Festival, 23 October 1929.

3 Fritz Theodore Albert Delius, c. 1865. Photograph *Coll.* Eric Fenby.

Joseph Joachim. Postcard photograph by Bassano.

4 Bradford in the later 1870s. Print in the collection of the Local Studies Department, City Library, Bradford.

The Old Bridge, Ilkley. Postcard photograph.

5 Ilkley Moor. Photograph *Coll.* R. Davies.

5 Fritz Delius, c. 1874. Photograph *Coll.* Eric Fenby.

Bradford Grammar School (later the Carlton School). Photograph by L. Carley, 1975.

6 A summer holiday début in 1879. Original in Leeds City Libraries.

W. G. Grace. Painting by Archibald Stuart-Wortley, 1890. Postcard.

The International College, at Isleworth. Photograph by L. Carley, 1975.

7 Stroud, c. 1880. Print in the collection of J. H. Stephens. Courtesy G. G. Hoare.

Hans Sitt. Postcard photograph.

Late nineteenth-century Chemnitz. Photograph. Courtesy Allgemeiner Deutscher Nachrichtendienst.

8 Emil Theodor Delius (1829–1898). Photograph by Erwin Hanfstaengl, Paris. *Coll.* Familienverbindung Delius, Bielefeld.

Monte-Carlo. Entrée du Casino, Jardins fleuris. Postcard photograph.

Saint-Étienne—Place du Peuple. Postcard photograph.

9 Stockholm at the turn of the century. Photograph. *Coll.* Stockholm Stadsmuseum.

Norrköping in 1876. Original lithograph in Norrköpings Museum. Courtesy Lars Arnö, Royal Swedish Embassy, London.

The Jotunheim Mountains. Picture Postcard from F.D. to Granville Bantock, 17 August 1908. Delius Trust.

10 Delius with his mother in 1884, shortly before leaving for America. Photograph. *Coll.* Eric Fenby.

Delius with Charles Douglas in 1884, shortly before leaving for America. Photograph. *Coll.* Eric Fenby.

The Cunard Liner *Gallia*. Painting in the collection of the Cunard Steam-Ship Co. Ltd.

11 Palm Trees, St. Johns River, Florida. Painting by Winslow Homer. *Coll.* Cummer Gallery of Art, Jacksonville. Courtesy Mr. and Mrs. John W. Donahoo, Jacksonville.

12 View of East Bay Street, Jacksonville, 1894. Photograph in the Florida Collection, Haydon Burns Library, Jacksonville.

St. Johns River Steamer 'City of Jacksonville' c. 1890. Photograph in the State Photograph Archives, Strozier Library, Florida State University.

The Delius House. Pen drawing by Virgil Dube. Courtesy Delius Association of Florida.

Panorama of Jacksonville from the St. Johns River, Florida, 1881. Original in the Florida Collection, Haydon Burns Library, Jacksonville.

12–13 Solana Grove. Photograph by L. Carley, 1972.

13 A page from a MS notebook dating from the Florida years, showing harmony exercises and sketches for a part-song. *Coll*: Jacksonville University.

Title page of *Zum Carnival Polka*, Delius's first published work. *Coll*: Library of Congress, Washington DC.

14 Blanche Rueckert. Photograph by A. H. Blunt, Danville, Va. Delius Trust Archive. Courtesy Mrs. Robert S. Gordon, Scarsdale, N.Y.

John Frederick Rueckert. Photograph by Faber and Friese, Norfolk, Va. Delius Trust Archive. Courtesy Mrs. Robert S. Gordon, Scarsdale, N.Y.

Gertrude Rueckert. Photograph by A. H. Blunt. Delius Trust Archive. Courtesy Mrs. Robert S. Gordon, Scarsdale, N.Y.

'Fritz Delius will begin . . .' Advertisement in the *Danville Register*, 3 October 1885. From the Newspaper Collection, Duke University Library, Durham, North Carolina. Courtesy Prof. William Randel.

'—Prof Fritz Delius assisted by . . .' from 'In a Nutshell', *Danville Register*, 6 October 1885. Duke University Library Newspaper Collection. Courtesy Prof. William Randel.

Roanoke Female College, c. 1883. *Coll.* Averett College Archives, Danville. Courtesy Miss Mary C. Fugate, Danville.

15 Delius performs at Danville. Programme of a concert at the Roanoke Female College, Danville, Va., preserved in a scrapbook in the R. S. Phifer Papers, Southern Historical Collection, University of North Carolina Library.

Virginia Ann Watkins. Photograph. *Coll.* Haydon Burns Library, Jacksonville.

Robert Phifer. Photograph. *Coll.* Haydon Burns Library, Jacksonville.

16 Leipzig: The Conservatorium. Postcard photograph.

Delius in Leipzig. Photograph. Atelier Herrmann. *Coll.* Grainger Museum, University of Melbourne.

A card party at Leipzig. Photograph. *Coll.* Grieg Museum, Troldhaugen.

17 Edvard Grieg. Postcard photograph by Whitlock.

Part of title page of autograph MS of *Paa Vidderne* (melodrama), 1888, with dedication to Grieg. Delius Trust Vol. 2.

18 Delius with four of his sisters, c. 1888. Photograph. *Coll.* Grainger Museum.

Title page of *5 Lieder aus dem Norwegischen*, Augener 8829, published 1890; Delius's first publication in England.

19 André Messager. Caricature by Gabriel Fauré. *Coll.* Bibliothèque Nationale, Paris. Courtesy Jean-Michel Nectoux.

Paris: The Opera. Postcard photograph.

20 Ville d'Avray: Corot's lake. Photograph by L. Carley, 1973.

Part of a page from the autograph MS of the early String Quartet. Delius Trust Vol. 35.

21 No. 8, Boulevard de la Mairie, Croissy. Photograph by L. Carley, 1973.

Java Programme. *Coll.* Eric Fenby.

Portrait of the violinist Arve Arvesen. Oil on canvas, c. 1887, by Edvard Munch. Private collection. Photograph courtesy of Munch Museum, Oslo.

22–23 Fritz Delius. 1) Profile drawing by Edvard Munch, published in *Verdens Gang*, Christiania, 12 October 1891. 2) Drawing by Edvard Munch in a book of sketches mainly made at Saint-Cloud, c. 1890. *Coll.* Munch Museum. I am indebted to Curator Arne Eggum for his assistance in identifying this drawing.

22 Bjørnstjerne Bjørnson. Postcard photograph.

Concert programme. Reprinted from Rachel Lowe: 'Delius's First Performance'. *The Musical Times*, March 1965, p. 191.

23 Fritz Delius. Pastel by Daniel de Monfreid, 1893. *Coll.* Derek Hudson.

Richard and Mildred Le Gallienne. Photograph in Richard Whittington-Egan and Geoffrey Smerdon: *The Quest for the Golden Boy*. Unicorn Press, London 1960.

24 Isidore de Lara in 1890. Photograph by Numa Blanc, Aix-les-Bains.

Princess Alice of Monaco. Photograph by Rosemont, Bradford.

25 Title page of *Anatomie et Physiologie de l'Orchestre*, Chamuel, Paris 1894.

Papus. Unattributed portrait in Philippe Encausse: *Papus, Dr. Gérard Encausse, sa vie, son oeuvre* (Paris 1932).

Caricature of Christian Sinding by Ottokar Nováček. Letter from Nováček to Delius, 18 May 1896. Delius Trust Archive.

26 No. 6, rue Vercingétorix. Photograph by Rafael Rådberg, 1912. Carlheim-Gyllensköld Collection, Royal Library Stockholm.

William Molard. Photograph. Courtesy of the late Dr. Gerda Kjellberg, Stockholm.

Madame Charlotte's crémerie. The panels to the left and right of the entrance were painted by Mucha and Slewinski respectively. Photograph, c. 1900, in the Carlheim-Gyllensköld Collection, Royal Library, Stockholm.

Paul Gauguin. Etching by Judith Ericson Molard [Judith Gérard], in Gilles Gérard-Arlberg: 'Nr 6, rue Vercingétorix', *Konstrevy*, 35, 2, Stockholm 1958.

27 Jelka Rosen and Ida Gerhardi at art class in Paris. Photograph. Courtesy Frau Malve Steinweg, Lüdenscheid.

Alphonse Mucha in 1897. Photograph. Courtesy Jiri Mucha.

28 Ida Molard in her studio. Photograph. Courtesy of the late Dr. Gerda Kjellberg, Stockholm.

At the rue Vercingétorix. Photograph, c. 1895 in Gilles Gérard-Arlberg: *op. cit.*

Julien Leclercq. Photograph in Julien Leclercq: *La Physionomie*, Paris 1896.

facing p. 28.

Slewinski with Bunch of Flowers by Paul Gauguin, oil on canvas c. 1891. *Coll.* National Museum of Western Art, Tokyo.

Nevermore, by Paul Gauguin. Oil on canvas. 1897. *Coll.* Courtauld Institute Galleries, London.

facing p. 29.

Edvard Munch: Self-portrait with cigarette. Oil on canvas, 1895. *Coll.* Munch Museum, Oslo.

29 Florent Schmitt. Woodcut in André Coeuroy: *La Musique française moderne*, Delagrave, Paris 1922.

A page from Florent Schmitt's MS vocal score of Delius's opera *The Magic Fountain*. Delius Trust Archive.

30 August Strindberg. Lithograph by Edvard Munch, 1896. *Coll.* Munch Museum.

A few bars from an autograph MS of Delius's setting of Verlaine's 'Le ciel est, par-dessus le toit' (1895). Delius Trust Vol. 48A.

Paul Verlaine on his deathbed. Photograph, 1896. Strindberg Collection. Royal Library, Stockholm.

31 Chemical analysis for gold effected on Strindberg's behalf. Delius Trust Archive.

Edvard Munch: Self-portrait with skeleton arm. Lithograph, 1895. *Coll.* Munch Museum.

32 Jelka Rosen. Oil on canvas, 1897, by Ida Gerhardi. *Coll.* Frau Malve Steinweg, Lüdenscheid.

Title page of *5 Chansons*, L. Grus, Paris, published 1896; Delius's first publication in France. *Coll.* Bibliothèque Nationale.

32–33 Grez-sur-Loing. View of the bridge. Postcard photograph in the Strindberg collection, Royal Library, Stockholm.

33 Jutta Bell. Photograph. *Coll.* Haydon Burns Library, Jacksonville.

Fragment of C. F. Keary's original MS libretto for *Koanga*. Delius Trust Vol. 39.

From Delius's MS sketches for *Koanga*. Delius Trust Vol. 39.

Bras-coupé (Koanga), from an engraving by Albert Herter. Photograph in Delius Trust Archive.

34 Jens Peter Jacobsen. Painting by Ernst Josephson, 1879. Photograph in Delius Trust Archive.

Part of first page of autograph MS of song *Black Roses* (1901). *Coll.* OUP archives.

Part of first page of autograph MS full score of *Seven Danish Songs* (1897). Delius Trust Vol. 12.

35 Ida Gerhardi: self-portrait, Paris 1903. Oil on canvas. *Coll.* Märkisches Museum, Witten.

Grez-sur-Loing: view from the bridge. Photograph by L. Carley 1973.

36 Gunnar Heiberg. Lithograph by Edvard Munch, 1896. *Coll.* Munch Museum.

Henrik Ibsen. Lithograph by Edvard Munch, 1902. *Coll.* Munch Museum.

37 Fritz Delius. Sketch by Christian Krohg in *Verdens Gang*, Oslo, 23 October 1897.

The Christiania Theatre. Photograph. *Coll.* L. Carley.

38 Hans Haym. Photograph. Courtesy Frau Marie-Luise Baum, Wuppertal.

A page from an autograph MS of the solo part of the Piano Concerto (1897). Delius Trust Vol. 10.

Ferruccio Busoni. Postcard engraving. Th. Weger, Leipzig.

39 Charlotte Bødtker Naeser. Photograph by Fotografia Central, V. Lopez G. Santiago. Delius Trust Archive.

Daniel de Monfreid: self-portrait. Sketch. Reprinted from Jean Loize: *Les Amitiés du peintre Georges-Daniel de Monfreid*. Chez Jean Loize, 1951.

Nevermore by Paul Gauguin. *See above.*

40 Gabriel Fauré by John Singer Sargent.

Letter from Fauré to Lady Lewis. [Spring 1899]. *Coll.* Pierpont Morgan Library, New York.

41 Handbill: Delius Orchestral Concert. *Coll.* Library of Congress.

John Singer Sargent (1897). Lithograph by William Rothenstein.

London's West End. Postcard photograph.

42 Delius in 1899. Photograph by Window and Grove, London. *Coll.* Christopher Brunel.

Concert review from the *Manchester Courier*, 31 May 1899.

Concert programme (St. James's Hall, 30 May 1899). *Coll.* Manuel Tarshish, White Plains, N.Y.

43 Delius in 1899. Photograph by Window and Grove, London. *Coll.* Christopher Brunel.

Andrew Black. Postcard photograph.

between pages 44 and 45

44 Paris: Pont Alexandre III. Postcard photograph.

Portion of MS sketches for *Paris*. Delius Trust Vol. 40.

Jelka Rosen by Ida Gerhardi. See 32n.

Frederick Delius. Oil on canvas, 1903, by Ida Gerhardi. *Coll.* Frau Malve Steinweg, Lüdenscheid.

Jelka Rosen. Oil on canvas, 1901, by Ida Gerhardi. *Coll.* Frau Malve Steinweg, Lüdenscheid. The picture also shows Jelka's cook Marie Blandel, and the pet jackdaw, 'Koanga'.

Garden. Oil on canvas, by Jelka Delius. n.d. *Coll.* Eric Fenby, London.

45 Jelka painting. Photograph. *Coll.* Frau Malve Steinweg, Lüdenscheid.

46 A page from Florent Schmitt's MS vocal score of Delius's opera *A Village Romeo and Juliet*. Delius Trust Vol. 19. The voice parts and English words are in Delius's own hand.

47 Richard Strauss. Photograph by E. O. Hoppe.

48 Maurice Ravel. Engraving 1909, by Achille Ouvré. *Coll.* Bibliothèque Nationale, Paris.

Part of a page from Maurice Ravel's MS vocal score of Delius's opera *Margot la Rouge*. Delius Trust Vol. 20. Delius has completed some bars left blank by Ravel.

49 The Violin Concert (Bella Edwards and Eva Mudocci). Lithograph, 1903, by Edvard Munch. *Coll.* Munch Museum.

50 Julius Buths. From Elgar's copy of the photograph. Courtesy Elgar Birthplace Trust.

51 Elberfeld: The Stadttheater. Unattributed pen drawing. Courtesy Frau Marie-Luise Baum.

Fritz Cassirer. Photograph. *Coll.* Claude Cassirer, Ohio.

Elberfeld: the monorail suspension railway. Postcard photograph.

Review dated 31 March 1904 from the *Täglicher Anzeiger*, Elberfeld. Courtesy Frau Marie-Luise Baum.

52 Elberfeld: general view. Postcard photograph.

Elberfeld: The Stadthalle. Postcard photograph.

53 Un bourgeois. Bronze by Auguste Rodin. *Coll.* Dr. M. Michaelis.

Auguste Rodin in his studio. Chalk sketch 1906, by Ida Gerhardi.

Sources of quotations

2 *My father loved* . . . F.D. quoted in HESELTINE, p. 3.
My mother was not . . .F.D. quoted in HESELTINE, p. 3.

3 *Delius, as a boy* . . . William Rothenstein, MEN AND MEMORIES, I, Faber (London: 1931), p. 10.
Julius Delius would . . . HESELTINE, p.6.
I cannot remember . . . F.D. quoted in HESELTINE, p. 5.

4 *I shall always think* . . . CLARE DELIUS, p. 273.
I loved riding . . . F.D. quoted in HESELTINE, p. 4.
When I was six . . . HESELTINE, p. 5.
The next great thrill . . . F.D. in conversation with Percy Grainger. Ms notes by Grainger now in the Grainger Museum, University of Melbourne.

5 *The Bradford Grammar School* . . . William Rothenstein, *Men and Memories*, I, Faber (London: 1931), pp. 7–8. Rothenstein attended the school some ten years after Delius.

6 *I saw a match* . . . F.D. in conversation with Percy Grainger (Grainger Museum Ms).
It was towards the end . . . CLARE DELIUS p. 53.
We always spent six weeks . . . F.D. in conversation with Percy Grainger (Grainger Museum Ms).

7 . . . *in Chemnitz* . . . HESELTINE, p. 8.

9 *The influence of the scenic grandeur* . . . BEECHAM, p. 21.

11 *I was also in the wilderness* . . . Letter to Philip Heseltine, 19 May 1918 (British Library Add. Mss. 52547–9).
I was demoralised . . . F.D. quoted in FENBY, p. 164.

12 *Negroes are certainly* . . . Letter [from Grez-sur-Loing] to Edward Elgar, 4 January 1934 (Worcestershire Archives).
The climate and the flowers . . . Letter [from Solana Grove] to Jelka Rosen, April 1897 (Grainger Museum).

13 *As far as my composing* . . . F.D. quoted in FENBY, p. 168.

15 *Mr. Fritz Delius charmed* . . .Mrs. Belle McGehee Phifer, widow of Robert Phifer, quoted in CLARE DELIUS, p. 87.
I . . . recall the talented young friend . . . Letter from Robert Phifer [Danville] to F.D., 27 July 1894 (Delius Trust).

16 *I have a quartett* . . . Letter [from Leipzig] to Gertrude Rueckert, 11 December 1886. (Delius Trust).

17 *I tell you frankly* . . . Letter [from St. Malo] to Edvard Grieg, August 1888 (Bergen Library). Original in German.
Your manuscripts were a pleasant surprise . . . Letter from Edvard Grieg [Leipzig] to F.D., 28 February 1888 (Delius Trust). Original in German.
Such a Christmas Eve! . . .Letter from Edvard Grieg [Leipzig] to Frants Beyer, 25 December 1887. Quoted from the Norwegian in BREVE FRA EDVARD GRIEG TIL FRANTS BEYER: 1872–1907, ed. Marie Beyer, Steenske Forlag, (Kristiania: 1923), pp. 86–87.
This English-American . . . Letter from Edvard Grieg [Leipzig] to Frants Beyer, 20 February 1888. Quoted from the Norwegian in BREVE (*see above*) p. 95.

18 *You cannot imagine* . . . Letter from Christian Sinding [Leipzig] to F.D., 9 April 1888 (Delius Trust). Original in German.

19 *I have now settled down* . . .Letter [from 43, rue Cambon, Paris] to Edvard Grieg, May 1888 (Bergen Library). Original in German.
André Messager, whom he frequently met . . . HESELTINE, p. 30.

20 *Last Saturday Arvesen* . . . Letter [from Paris] to Edvard Grieg, February 1889 (Bergen Library). Original in German.
And you have written . . . Letter from Edvard Grieg [Bergen] to F.D., 30 December 1888 (Delius Trust). Original in German.
I have been in Ville d'Avray . . . Letter [from the Chalet des Lilas, à la Chaumière, Ville d'Avray] to Edvard Grieg, late 1888 (Bergen Library). Original in German.

21 *I have a suggestion* . . . Letter [from Ville d'Avray] to Edvard Grieg, January 1889 (Bergen Library). Original in German.

22 *I have always admired you* . . . Letter from Christian Sinding [Christiania] to F.D., 16 April 1891 (Delius Trust). Original in German.
I arrived here yesterday . . . Letter [from Fredriksvaern, Norway] to Edvard Grieg, 16 July 1891 (Bergen Library). Original in German.
I have just got one of your guests . . . Letter from Edvard Grieg [Troldhaugen] to Bjørnstjerne Bjørnson, 23 July 1891. Quoted from the Norwegian in BREVE FRA GRIEG: ET UDVALG VED GUNNAR HAUCH, Nordisk Forlag (Copenhagen: 1922) p. 86.

23 *We liked him much* . . . Letter from Richard Le Gallienne [Hanwell, Middlesex] to his mother, 27 February 1892. Quoted in Richard Whittington-Egan and Geoffrey Smerdon, THE QUEST OF THE GOLDEN BOY: THE LIFE AND LETTERS OF RICHARD LE GALLIENNE The Unicorn Press (London: 1960) p. 188.
I am very fond of it . . . Letter from Jelka Delius [Grez-sur-Loing] to Adine O'Neill, 8 January 1928 (Delius Trust).
Our friend Daniel . . . Letter from William Molard [Eygurande, Corrèze, France] to F.D., 5 September 1901 (Delius Trust). Original in French.

24 *The Princess Brancaccia* . . . Isidore de Lara [Paris] to F.D., 13 May 1893 (Delius Trust).
Let me tell you how fine . . . Letter from Alice, Princess of Monaco, to F.D., 26 February 1894 (Delius Trust). [in English].
The seventh international concert . . . Review of Monte Carlo concert in LE FIGARO, 2 March 1894, p. 3. Original in French.

25 *Thank you for your* . . . Letter from Ottokar Nováček to F.D., 7 May 1896 (Delius Trust). Original in German.
How are you getting on . . . Letter from Christian Sinding [Drøbak, Norway] to F.D., 11 September 1894 (Delius Trust). Original in German.

26 *I met Strindberg at the studio* . . . F.D., quoted in HESELTINE, p. 31. (Note: Delius writes, inaccurately, *Eriksen, Mollard*).
Among the habitués . . . F.D., quoted in HESELTINE, p. 31 (Note: Delius writes *Leclerc, Slivinsky* in original).
. . . *in addition to being our eating place* . . . Alphonse Mucha, quoted in Jiri Mucha: ALPHONSE MUCHA—HIS LIFE AND ART, Heinemann, London 1966, p. 92.

28 *He looks as if he had just stepped* . . . Ernest Dowson speaking with Aubrey Beardsley, quoted in ERNEST DOWSON by Mark Longaker. University of Pennsylvania Press, Philadephia, 1945, p. 186.
There is a man named Leclercq . . . Letter to Jutta Bell-Ranske, August 1894 (Jacksonville University).
[Gauguin] did not bear the mark . . . Judith Gérard on Gauguin: [LA PETITE FILLE ET LE TUPAPAU: MANAO TUPAPAU. From a copy of the original French ms in the collection of Bengt Danielsson.]

29 *Schmitt is busy working* . . . Letter from Léon Moreau [Paris] to F.D., 22 May 1894 (Delius Trust). Original in French.
I was most impressed . . . Letter from Christian Sinding [Christiania] to F.D., 25 June 1895 (Delius Trust). Original in German.
I have a vague idea . . . Letter [from 33 rue Ducouëdic, Paris] to Jutta Bell-Ranske, 29 July 1894 (Jacksonville University).
I should . . . *like to give* . . . Letter [from 33 rue Ducouëdic, Paris] to Jutta Bell-Ranske, 29 May 1894 (Jacksonville University).

30 . . . *his growing power* . . . BEECHAM, p. 83.
He was a remarkable person . . . Alphonse Mucha on Strindberg. [Quoted in Jiri Mucha: ALPHONSE MUCHA—HIS LIFE AND ART, Heinemann, London, 1966, p. 154].
Shortly after Paul Verlaine . . . F.D. quoted in HESELTINE, p. 33.

31 *I don't see many Norwegians* . . . Letter [from 33 rue Ducouëdic, Paris] to Randi Blehr, 8 December 1896 (State Archives, Oslo). Original in German.
Strindberg . . . *was also occupied with alchemy* . . . F.D. quoted in HESELTINE, p. 32.
He was constantly imagining . . . F.D. quoted in HESELTINE, p. 34.
The gas apparatus seems to be based . . . Postcard from August Strindberg to Edvard Munch, Paris 19 July 1896. Quoted from the Swedish in STRINDBERGS BREV, XI, MAJ 1895—NOVEMBER 1896. Utgivna av Torsten Eklund. Bonniers, Stockholm 1969, p. 277.

32 *Dear Miss Rosen/I thank you very much* . . . First letter from F.D. to Jelka Rosen [from 33 rue Ducouëdic, Paris], 1 March 1896. From a transcript in the Delius Trust Archive; original in the Grainger Museum.
The village is situated where the plateau slopes . . . Description of Grez-sur-Loing by August Strindberg. From BLAND FRANSKA BÖNDER, Bonniers, Stockholm, 1889. Original in Swedish.
A place like this . . . F.D., quoted by Jelka Delius in BEECHAM, p. 83.
Your description of Grez . . . Letter [from Haugen, S/Aurdal, Valders, Norway] to Jelka Rosen, end of June 1896. From a transcript in the Delius Trust Archive; original in the Grainger Museum.
A low bridge of many arches . . . Robert Louis Stevenson on Grez-sur-Loing, in a letter to his mother from Barbizon, August 1875. From THE LETTERS OF ROBERT LOUIS STEVENSON TO HIS FAMILY AND FRIENDS, Methuen, London, 1900, vol. I, p. 104.

33 *I dont believe in realism* . . . Letter [from 33 rue Ducouëdic, Paris] to Jutta Bell-Ranske, 25 February 1896 (Jacksonville University).
I am writing another opéra . . . Letter [from 33 rue Ducouëdic, Paris] to Jutta Bell-Ranske, 9 February 1896 (Jacksonville University).
At present all goes well . . . Letter [from Haugen, S/Aurdal, Valders, Norway] to Jutta Bell-Ranske, 15 July 1896 (Jacksonville University).

34 *Je ne vois guère à retenir après cela* . . . Claude Debussy on the Seven Danish Songs, given at the Société Nationale, conductor Vincent d'Indy, soloist Christianne Andray, 16 March 1901. From LA REVUE BLANCHE, Paris, 1 April 1901, vol XXIV No. 188, p. 551.
I have written 5 songs . . . Letter [from Claremont, Bradford] to Jutta Bell-Ranske, December 1896 (Jacksonville University).

35 *Although I speak without* . . . Letter from Ida Gerhardi [Grez] to her brother, 20 September 1897. Original in German.

36 *No one speaks any more* . . . Letter [from Holmenkollens Turisthotel, Norway] to Jelka Rosen, end of October 1897. (Grainger Museum).

37 *Delius* . . . *has certainly had a real success* . . . Letter from William Molard [Paris] to Edvard Munch. 7 March 1898 (Munch Museum). Original in Norwegian.
Are you working on anything . . . F.D. is interviewed by Christian Krohg in Verdens Gang, Christiania, 23 October 1897.

38 *I am spending a lot of time* . . . Letter [from 33 rue Ducouëdic, Paris] to Jelka Rosen, January 1898. (Grainger Museum).
The opening evoked interest . . . Review of 1st performance of *Over the Hills and far away*, conducted by Hans Haym, *Täglicher Anzeiger*, Elberfeld, 16 November 1897. Original in German.

39 *Tuesday 8 November 1898* . . . *Delius comes* . . . Extract from the unpublished notebooks of Daniel de Monfreid, in the possession of Mme. A Joly-Segalen, Bourg-la-Reine, France. Original in French.
Friday 11 November 1898. At 11 o'clock Delius visits . . . (ibid).
You did well to let Delius . . . Letter from Paul Gauguin [Tahiti] to Daniel de Monfreid, 12 January 1899 [LETTRES DE GAUGUIN À DANIEL DE MONFREID. Ed. Mme. Joly-Segalen. Georges Falaize, Paris, 1950, p. 135.] Original in French.
I am glad you don't disapprove . . . Letter from Daniel de Monfreid [St. Clément] to Paul Gauguin, 11 march 1899 [LETTRES, etc. p. 211]. Original in French.
I send you this picture . . . Letter from Charlotte Bødtker Naeser, Norwegian pianist (later Charlotte Winter-Hjelm) [San Bernardo, Chile] to F.D. 21 March 1898. (Delius Trust). [in English].

40 *Gabriel Fauré and a few of the best* . . . Letter [from Paris] to Jelka Rosen, March 1899. (Grainger Museum).

41 *It is very kind of you* . . . Letter from John Singer Sargent [London] to F.D., May 1899. (Delius Trust).
I don't hope for any success . . . Letter [from Pagani's, London] to Jelka Rosen, 7 May 1899 (Grainger Museum).
Lady Lewis has allowed me . . . Letter from John Singer Sargent [London] to F.D. 1899. (Delius Trust).

42 *The Concert of course has done* . . . Letter [from Grez-sur-Loing] to Jutta Bell-Ranske, June 1899 (Jacksonville University).
Your success in London . . . Letter from Edvard Munch [Aasgaardstrand] to F.D., 24 June 1899 (Delius Trust). Original in Norwegian.

43 *I see Fritz* . . . Julius Delius, quoted in CLARE DELIUS, p. 131.
Delius fought against . . . Notes by Mrs. Adey Brunel, on the back of one of the photographs taken on this occasion (Coll. Christopher Brunel, London).
. . . *more money for you* . . . Letter from Mrs. Julius Delius [Bradford] to her son, 13 January 1900. (Delius Trust).
I saw Hansen today . . . Letter [from Copenhagen] to Jelka Rosen, 14 August 1899 (Grainger Museum).

44 *In parts I find the piece* . . . Letter from Julius Buths [Düsseldorf] to F.D., 26 July 1903. (Delius Trust). Original in German.
If only all the bizarre . . . Review of the first performance of *Paris*, *Täglicher Anzeiger*. Elberfeld, 15 December 1901. Original in German.

45 . . . *the little garden pleases* . . . Letter from Achille Ouvré to Frederick and Jelka Delius, 7 October 1907, on Jelka's pictures at the *Salon* (Delius Trust). Original in French.
You give generously to me of your soul . . . Letter from Auguste Rodin [Paris] to Jelka Rosen, 15 March 1901. (Delius Trust). Original in French.
The lilacs are in bud . . . Letter from Jelka Rosen [Grez] to Auguste Rodin, 28 April 1901 (Musée Rodin, Paris). Original in French.
I think of our fresh morning walk . . . Letter from Jelka Rosen [Paris] to Auguste Rodin, 7 February 1902 (Musée Rodin). Original in French.

46 *I am sick of losing time* . . . Letter [from Berlin] to Jelka Rosen, February/March 1901 (Grainger Museum).
When I have done here . . . *My second act* . . . Letters [from Berlin] to Jelka Rosen, January 1901 and 14 March 1901 (Grainger Museum).

47 *I have read your score* . . . Letter from Richard Strauss [Charlottenburg] to F.D., 2 March 1902 (Delius Trust). Original in German.
'Paris' for two pianos . . . Letter from Julius Buths [Düsseldorf] to F.D., 24 June 1903 (Delius Trust). Original in German.
Last Friday we played . . . Letter from Julius Buths [Düsseldorf] to F.D., 19 July 1903 (Delius Trust). Original in German.

48 *I have transcribed literally* . . . Letter from Maurice Ravel [St. Jean-de-Luz] to F.D., 3 October 1902 (Delius Trust). Original in French.
The transcription is well under way . . . Letter from Maurice Ravel [St. Jean-de-Luz] to F.D., 10 September 1902 (Delius Trust). Original in French.

49 *I am going to stay outside* . . . Letter from Edvard Munch [Leipzig] to his aunt, Karen Bjølstad, 27 February 1903. From EDVARD MUNCHS BREV. FAMILIEN. Et udvalg ved Inger Munch. Munch museets skrifter, I, Oslo 1949. Original in Norwegian.
I should like to stay . . . Letter from Edvard Munch [Charlottenburg] to F.D., 30 January 1903 (Delius Trust). Original in German.
Young Munk . . . Letter from Jelka Rosen [Grez] to Auguste Rodin, 12 March 1903 (Musée Rodin). Original in French.
Please tell me . . . Letter from Edvard Munch [Berlin] to F.D., February 1905 (Delius Trust). Original in German.
Miss Eva Mudocci . . . Letter [from Grez] to Edvard Munch, 11 February 1905 (Munch Museum). Original in German.
You asked about Delius . . . Letter from Eva Mudocci [Paris], to Edvard Munch, 12 December [1905?] (Munch Museum). Original in German.

50 My *Mitternachtslied* . . . Letter [from Grez] to Edvard Grieg, 28 September 1903 (Bergen Library). Original in German.
I have just come back . . . Letter [from Grez] to Edvard Grieg, summer 1903 (Bergen Library). Original in German.
Your new work . . . Letter from Julius Buths [Düsseldorf] to F.D., 26 July 1903 (Delius Trust). Original in German.
On the 25th I married . . . Letter [from Grez] to Edvard Grieg, 28 September 1903. (Bergen Library). Original in German.
. . . *now we are to be married* . . . Letter from Jelka Rosen [Grez] to Auguste Rodin, 14 September 1903 (Musée Rodin). Original in French.
[Delius] the man who has . . . Letter from Julius Buths [Düsseldorf] to F.D., 26 July 1903 (Delius Trust). Original in German.

You have now reached . . . Letter from Edvard Grieg [Hotel Westminster, Christiania] to F.D., 23 October 1903 (Delius Trust). Original in German.

51 *While I was in Elberfeld* . . . CLARE DELIUS, p. 148.

52 *. . . this dismal town* . . . Letter from Jelka Delius [Elberfeld] to Auguste Rodin, 27 February 1904 (Musée Rodin). Original in French.
Something like a war . . . Review of 'Delius Concert' of 24 October 1904 in Elberfeld, TÄGLICHER ANZEIGER, 26 October 1904. Original in German.
Please convey to Mr. Delius . . . Letter from Auguste Rodin [Paris] to Jelka Delius, 9 December 1904 (Delius Trust). Original in French.
[Appalachia] is not over-extravagant . . . Review by Friedrich Kerst of the first performance of *Appalachia*. TÄGLICHER ANZEIGER, Elberfeld, 18 October 1904. Original in German.
He has a more acute ear . . . Hans Haym, on *Appalachia*, in the TÄGLICHER ANZEIGER, Elberfeld, 1904 (Undated cutting). Original in German.

53 *The music of Delius* . . . Letter from Jelka Delius [Elberfeld] to Auguste Rodin, 27 February 1904 (Musée Rodin). Original in French.
You will never be able . . . Letter from Jelka Delius [Paris] to Auguste Rodin, 16 November 1904 (Musée Rodin). Original in French.
I must see you . . . Letter from Auguste Rodin [Paris] to F.D., 22 October 1902 (Delius Trust). Original in French.
I intend to arrange . . . Draft for a letter from Edvard Munch to F.D., n.d. [April 1906] (Munch Museum). Original in German.

54 *Seadrift has made* . . . Letter from Hans Haym to F.D., 1 June 1906 (Delius Trust). Original in German.
. . . a work of a depressing despair . . . Review by G. Altmann of the first performance of *Sea Drift* in Essen 1906. DIE MUSIK, V, 19, Erstes Juliheft, 1905/1906 p. 50. Original in German.
Accept these brief thanks . . . Letter from Max Schillings [Munich] to F.D., 21 July 1906 (Delius Trust). Original in German.
Now all this time . . . Letter from Carl Schuricht [Goslar] to F.D., 12 March 1908 (Delius Trust). Original in German.

56 *I stand in awe* . . . Letter from Max Schillings [Munich] to F.D., 16 November 1906 (Delius Trust). Original in German.
. . . sufficiently well-known . . . Review by Eduard Wahl of first performance of parts of *A Mass of Life* in Munich, June 1908, in DIE MUSK, VII, 20, Zweites Juliheft, 1907/1908 p. 98. Original in German.
I thank you for having . . . Letter from Hans Haym [Elberfeld] to F.D., 20 July 1909 (Delius Trust). Original in German.
So, you foul pagan . . . Letter from William Molard [Paris] to F.D., 5 May 1908 (Delius Trust). Original in French.

57 *I consider Nietzsche* . . . Letter to Philip Heseltine, 23 June 1912 (BL Add. MSS. 52547-9).

58 *He carefully calls his work* . . . Review of first performance of *A Village Romeo and Juliet* in Berlin, 1907. DIE MUSIK, VI, 12, Jahr 1906/1907. Zweites Märzheft. p. 375. Original in German.
'A Village Romeo and Juliet' made an excellent . . . Letter from Engelbert Humperdinck [Berlin] to F.D., 12 March 1907 (Delius Trust). Original in German.

59 *I send you today* . . . Letter [from Grez] to John Coates, 16 December 1907 (Coll. Albi Rosenthal).
Welcome to England . . . Letter from John Coates [London] to F.D., 25 April 1907 (Delius Trust).
It would be worth while . . . Letter [from London] to Jelka Delius, 15 April 1907 (Grainger Museum).

60 *I never told you* . . . Letter from Percy Grainger [Veendam] to F.D., 26 January 1911 (Library of Congress transcript).
My star has been most successful . . . Letter [from London] to Jelka Delius, 21 April 1907 (Grainger Museum).
The feeling of nature . . . Letter [from Grez] to Percy Grainger, 10 June 1907 (Coll. Percy Grainger Library Society, White Plains, New York).
I consider Percy Grainger . . . Letter to Philip Heseltine, 23 June 1912 (BL Add. MSS 52547-9).

61 *I did not think* . . . Letter from Robin Legge [London, after first British performance of Piano Concerto], 22 October 1907 (Delius Trust).
I should so much like . . . Letter from Ralph Vaughan Williams [13 Cheyne Walk] to F.D., n.d. [late October 1907] (Delius Trust).

62 *The first performance in England* . . . BEECHAM, p. 146.
There is something noble . . . Letter from Havergal Brian [Hartshill, Stoke-on-Trent] to F.D., 14 November 1908 (Delius Trust).
I've been going through . . . Letter from Havergal Brian [Hartshill, Stoke-on-Trent] to F.D., 22 December 1907 (Delius Trust).
Rarely has a British composer . . . Review of first British performance of *Appalachia* (unattributed), quoted in CLARE DELIUS, p. 161.

63 *[Beecham] is wonderfully gifted* . . . Letter [from Grez] to Ethel Smyth, 17 February 1909 (Ethel Smyth, BEECHAM AND PHARAOH, Chapman and Hall, London 1935 p. 26).
I know there are spendidly musical . . . Letter [from Grez] to Granville Bantock, 16 March 1909 (Delius Trust).
I am trying to arrange . . . Letter from Thomas Beecham [Boreham Wood] to F.D., 3 June 1908 (Delius Trust).
Sincerest congratulations . . . Letter from Henry J. Wood [London] to F.D., 2 July 1908 (Delius Trust).

65 *I was quite cool* . . . Letter [from London?] to Jelka Delius, 12 December 1908 (Grainger Museum).
I conducted without a catastrophe . . . Letter [from Grez] to Granville Bantock, 17 December 1908 (Delius Trust).
Boston: At the Symphony Concert . . . Review of 1909 concert in Boston, Mass., USA, by Louis C. Elson, in DIE MUSIK, IX, 19, Erstes Juliheft 1909/1910, p. 54. Original in German.

66 *Our publisher insists* . . . Letter from Zoltan Kodály to F.D., n.d. [1910] (Delius Trust). Original in German.
I am so alone here . . . Letter from Béla Bartók [Budapest], 7 June 1910 (typed transcript in Delius Trust Archive). Original in German.
For us the most important . . . Letter from Béla Bartók [Zürich] to Etelka Freund, 31 May 1910. (Quoted in BÉLA BARTÓK LETTERS, edited and annotated by János Demény (English translation), Faber, London, 1971, p. 104).

67 *I can write and tell you* . . . Letter from Béla Bartók [Budapest] to F.D., 27 March 1911 (typed transcript in Delius Trust Archive). Original in German.
. . . music should be . . . flowing . . . Letter [from Grez] to Béla Bartók, 13 August 1910 (Bartók Archive, Budapest). Original in German.
We are about to return . . . Picture postcard from Béla Bartók and Zoltan Kodály [Vienna] to F.D., February 1911 (Delius Trust). Original in German.

68 *Fred is now very much better* . . . Letter from Jelka Delius [Grez] to Adine O'Neill, 29 March 1911 (Delius Trust).

69 *It is of no importance* . . . Letter to Philip Heseltine, February 1912 (Quoted in Cecil Gray: PETER WARLOCK: A MEMOIR OF PHILIP HESELTINE, Cape, London, 1934, p. 46).
I cannot adequately express in words . . . Letter from Philip Heseltine [Eton College] to F.D., 17 June 1911 (Quoted in Cecil Gray: PETER WARLOCK, p. 39).
I spend most of my time . . . Letter from Philip Heseltine [Montgomery] to Colin Taylor, 1 August 1914 (Quoted in Cecil Gray: PETER WARLOCK, p. 58).
The Musical League I suppose . . . Letter [from Grez] to Granville Bantock, 11 April 1911 (Delius Trust).

I am afraid it is quite impossible . . . Letter [from Grez] to Igor Stravinsky, 27 May 1913 (Quoted in E. W. White: STRAVINSKY, THE COMPOSER AND HIS WORKS, Faber, London 1966, p. 550). Original in French.
I met Frederick Delius . . . Igor Stravinsky and Robert Craft, MEMORIES AND COMMENTARIES, Faber, London, 1960, p. 133n.)

70 *I should love to see* . . . Letter from Jelka Delius [Grez] to Marie Clews, 20 June 1916 (Delius Trust).

71 *. . . we are happy indeed* . . . Letter from Jelka Delius [Grez] to Marie Clews, 11 May 1916 (Delius Trust).

73 *Quite apart from my efforts* . . . Letter from Percy Grainger [New York] to F.D., 19 June 1915 (Library of Congress transcript).
. . . for the last week . . . Letter from Leopold Stokowski [Seal Harbour, Me.] to Andrew Wheeler, 25 September 1916 (transcript in the Delius Trust Archive).
I have been very troubled . . . Letter from Jelka Delius [Grez] to Marie Clews, 23 July 1917 (Delius Trust).
Fred has been working splendidly . . . Letter from Jelka Delius [Biarritz] to Marie Clews, 30 July 1918 (Delius Trust).
During the war I wrote . . . Letter [from London] to Ernest Newman, 31 January 1919 (Delius Trust).
Maud Cunard wrote me . . . Letter [from Grez] to Henry and Marie Clews, 21 August 1918 (Delius Trust).

74 *Delius has come back* . . . Letter from Ferruccio Busoni [London] to his wife, 23 November 1919 (Ferruccio Busoni: LETTERS TO HIS WIFE. Translated by Rosamond Ley, Edward Arnold, London, 1938, p. 287).
In Frankfort we stayed a month . . . Letter from Jelka Delius [Grez] to Marie Clews, 2 November 1919 (Delius Trust).
Length and cumbrousness, in my opinion . . . Quoted in CLARE DELIUS p. 199.

75 *In sum, a pastel* . . . Review of the first performance of *Fennimore and Gerda* in Frankfurt on 21 October 1919. (Undated cutting from the FRANKFURTER ZEITUNG in Delius Trust Archive). Original in German.
A final word on the non-lyrical nature . . . BEECHAM, p. 165.

76 *Lady C had* . . . Letter from Jelka Delius [Lesjaskog] to Marie Clews, 31 July 1921 (Delius Trust).
He has not been so very well . . . Letter from Jelka Delius to Philip Heseltine, 14 June 1920 (BL Add. MSS 52547-9).
I am so glad that I have seen you . . . Draft for a letter from Edvard Munch to F.D., n.d. (Munch Museum). Original in German.
If you meet Delius . . . Letter from Jappe Nilssen to Edward Munch at Wiesbaden, 10 May 1922 (From EDVARD MUNCHS KRISEÅR: with an introduction by Erna Holmboe Bang. Gyldendal, Norsk Forlag, 1963, p. 93). Original in Norwegian.

77 *I am sending you a little collection* . . . Letter from Jelka Delius [Grez] to Percy Grainger, 29 November 1923 (Delius Trust Archive transcript).
It is rather a physical breakdown . . . Letter from Jelka Delius [Mølmen Hotel, Lesjaskog, Gudbrandsdalen, Norway] to Adine O'Neill, 2 July 1922 (Delius Trust).

78 *There is really only one* . . . Letter to Philip Heseltine, 27 May 1917 (BL Add. MSS. 52547-9).

82 *I, myself, am entirely at a loss* . . . Letter [from Biarritz] to Philip Heseltine, 3 July 1918 (BL Add. MSS 52547-9).
Music is a cry of the soul . . . F.D. 'At the cross roads', THE SACKBUT, I, 5, Sept. 1920, p. 205.
. . . we are here in quite a media[e]val house . . . Letter from Jelka Delius [Frankfurt] to Henry and Marie Clews, 23 January 1923 (Delius Trust).
I am sorry the winter . . . Letter from Jelka Delius [Frankfurt] to Adine O'Neill, 30 March 1923 (Delius Trust).

81 *We were 9 days in London* . . . Letter [from Grez] to Percy Grainger, 29 September 1923 (Delius Trust Archive transcript).
When we were in London . . . Letter from Jelka Delius [Grez] to Percy Grainger, 14

October 1923 (Delius Trust Archive transcript).
It has been a great success . . . Letter from Jelka Delius [Grez] to Marie Clews, 27 October 1923 (Delius Trust).

82 *We were wondering, whether ever* . . . Letter [from Rapallo] to Percy Grainger, 23 January 1924 (Delius Trust Archive transcript).
It is beastly cold here now . . . Letter from Jelka Delius [Grez] to Percy Grainger, 29 November 1923 (Delius Trust Archive transcript).

83 *Fred loves the idea* . . . Letter from Jelka Delius [Rapallo] to Marie Clews, 5 March 1924 (Delius Trust).
We enjoyed being near you . . . Letter from Jelka Delius [Chalons-sur-Saône] to Henry and Marie Clews, 27 April 1924 (Delius Trust).

84 *Delius was a ghost* . . . Catherine Barjansky, PORTRAITS WITH BACKGROUNDS, Geoffrey Bles, London 1948, p. 96.
I had some wax with me . . . ibid. p. 98.
I have thought of you often . . . Letter from Jelka Delius [Grez] to Marie Clews, 31 August 1925 (Delius Trust).

85 *. . . the conceit that I could help* . . . [Eric Fenby, in the summer of 1928] FENBY, pp. 8-9.
I am greatly touched . . . Letter [from Grez] to Eric Fenby, 29 August 1928 (Delius Trust).
We are . . . living . . . Letter from Jelka Delius [Grez] to Marie Clews, 22 January 1928 (Delius Trust).
As to the Radio . . . Letter from Jelka Delius [Grez] to Marie Clews, 29 April 1929 (Delius Trust).
. . . Fred has been made . . . Letter from Jelka Delius [Grez] to Marie Clews, 8 April 1929 (Delius Trust).

87 *He is quite well* . . . Letter from Jelka Delius [Grez] to Eric Fenby, 22 December 1929 (Delius Trust).
Thank you for the very fine . . . From Delius's speech after the final concert of the 1929 Festival, quoted in CLARE DELIUS, p. 223.
He has been more lively . . . Letter from Jelka Delius [Grez] to Percy Grainger, 4 November 1930 (Delius Trust Archive transcript).

88 *After the 3rd Violin Sonata* . . . Letter from Jelka Delius [Grez] to Ernest Newman, 28 October 1930 (Delius Trust).

89 *When I look at him* . . . Letter from Jelka Delius [Grez] to Edvard Munch, 19 November 1928 (Munch Museum, Oslo). Original in German.
I have thought about making . . . Draft for a letter from Edvard Munch to F.D., n.d. [Spring 1929] (Munch Museum). Original in German.
I am sending you a beautiful photo . . . Letter from Jelka Delius [Grez] to Eric Fenby, 2 February 1932 (Delius Trust).
We are now all the time . . . Letter from Jelka Delius [Grez] to Percy Grainger, 17 March 1932 (Delius Trust Archive transcript).

90 *He would sit down* . . . Philip Oyler in SONS OF THE GENEROUS EARTH, Hodder and Stoughton, London 1963, pp. 53-4.
I have now got . . . Letter from Jelka Delius [Grez] to Henry and Marie Clews, 23 December 1931 (Delius Trust).
Not being able to see . . . F.D. quoted in FENBY, p. 73.
I am supposed to be improving . . . Letter from Sir Edward Elgar [nursing home] to F.D., 13 October 1933. (Delius Trust Archive transcript).
I still have a vivid memory . . . Letter from Sir Edward Elgar [Marl Bank, Worcester] to F.D., 1 July 1933 (Delius Trust Archive transcript).
His visit to me here . . . Letter [from Grez] to Ernest Newman, 13 December 1933 (Delius Trust).
When am I to have . . . Letter [from Grez] to Sir Thomas Beecham, 17 December 1933 (Delius Trust).

93 *The most precious part* . . . from Sir Thomas Beecham's funeral oration at Limpsfield, quoted in CLARE DELIUS, p. 277.